NOV 2 0
17

Wedding

HACKS

500+ WAYS TO STICK TO YOUR BUDGET, STAY STRESS-FREE, AND *Plan the Best Wedding Ever!*

MADDIE EISENHART

Adams
New York   London   Tor

Adams Media

An Imprint of Simon & Schuster, Inc.

57 Littlefield Street

Avon, Massachusetts 02322

Copyright © 2020 by
Simon & Schuster, Inc.

First Adams Media hardcover edition
November 2020

ADAMS MEDIA and colophon are
trademarks of Simon & Schuster.

For information about special
discounts for bulk purchases, please
contact Simon & Schuster Special
Sales at 1-866-506-1949 or
business@simonandschuster.com.

The Simon & Schuster Speakers
Bureau can bring authors to your live
event. For more information or to
book an event contact the Simon
& Schuster Speakers Bureau at
1-866-248-3049 or visit our website
at www.simonspeakers.com.

Interior design by Julia Jacintho
Illustrations and hand lettering by
Priscilla Yuen

Manufactured in the
United States of America

10 9 8 7 6 5 4 3 2 1

Library of Congress Cataloging-in-
Publication Data
Names: Eisenhart, Maddie, author.
Title: Wedding hacks / Maddie
Eisenhart.
Description: Avon, Massachusetts:
Adams Media, 2020. | Series: Hacks
| Includes index.
Identifiers: LCCN 2020034717 |
ISBN 9781507214053 (hc) |
ISBN 9781507214060 (ebook)
Subjects: LCSH:
Weddings--Planning.
Classification: LCC HQ745 .E37
2020 | DDC 395.2/2--dc23
LC record available at
https://lccn.loc.gov/2020034717

ISBN 978-1-5072-1405-3
ISBN 978-1-5072-1406-0 (ebook)

Contents

Acknowledgments

If I had known even a fraction of the information in this book when I got married, I would have saved so much time, money, and tears. Thank you, Adams Media, for letting me put ten years' worth of knowledge and experience into something that will help couples avoid my novice mistakes.

A huge debt of gratitude is owed to Jessi Rutherford of Sentimental Fools Events (Baltimore, Maryland), Jordan A. Maney of All The Days (San Antonio, Texas), and Cindy Savage of Aisle Less Traveled, *Super Gay Wedding* podcast, and *Choose Your Own Wedding* (Seattle, Washington) for their invaluable insights as professional wedding planners. If you want smart, funny, experienced professionals in your corner on your wedding day, you would do well to hire one of these brilliant humans. Thank you also to Erin Dodd and Genevieve Dreizen for witnessing as many weddings as they have in order to provide such wise, witty contributions to this book. And to Kate Bolen for being my first reader and most trusted editor.

Lastly, my deepest appreciation goes to my family. Michael, none of this would have happened without your crazy notion to get married before either of us could legally rent a car. Lincoln, you made this project possible and worthwhile in so many ways. And, of course, to my mother, who agreed to let me dress up as a bride for my fifth birthday (my idea, not hers), thus sparking a lifelong interest in weddings and marriage.

And to anyone who read this book and felt a little calmer afterward—you made it all worth it.

Introduction

Congratulations, you're getting hitched! Making it official. Tying the knot. While a wedding might be cause for celebration, the planning process isn't always confetti cannons and champagne toasts. Luckily *Wedding Hacks* is here to help you create an amazing big day.

Wedding Hacks is designed to be your pocket wedding planner—combining more than five hundred insider tips with practical advice for keeping your cool in the face of impractical expectations, family drama, and financial realities. This book will take you step-by-step through the planning process, from celebrating your engagement to kicking back on your honeymoon—saving you time, money, and stress along the way. You'll also learn how to avoid common wedding planning mistakes that could come back to haunt you later.

With *Wedding Hacks*, the planning process is covered from start to finish, so no matter where you are in your timeline you can jump right in and get the advice you need. So grab your partner and let's hack your way to the best wedding ever!

CHAPTER 1

Organizing Your Budget and To-Do List

1.

Wait a minute before you plan. It's tempting to jump right in to booking a venue and picking your outfits the minute you're engaged, but hold off on making any major decisions until you have some big conversations with your partner (and families) about budgets and expectations. You can't book a venue if you don't know how much you're spending, and you'll want to know in advance if any of your parents have unspoken expectations about the formality or size of your wedding. (They don't necessarily get to dictate those details, but their opinions will factor into your planning one way or another.)

2.

Prepare yourself for sticker shock. The weddings we've seen in movies and TV are incredibly expensive. Most of them feature details that cost more than your whole catering budget, so one of the first reactions you're likely to have while wedding planning is sticker shock. It's helpful to remember that unrealistic expectations aren't your fault (those on-screen weddings seemed so reasonable!) and sticker shock is normal. Start planning armed with this information and you're less likely to get your hopes up about the affordability of a five-tiered wedding cake.

3.

Say No! Most wedding "traditions" aren't that traditional at all (you'd be surprised how many are pop culture or marketing inventions), so eliminate anything that isn't essential. Take a pause before making any major wedding planning decisions and ask yourselves, "Is this really what *we* want?" and give a hard no to anything that doesn't fit.

4.

Research real wedding budgets. One of the most useful tools when you're trying to plan a wedding is seeing how other couples did it first. *Reddit*'s Weddings Under 10K forum and APracticalWedding.com's Real Weddings both share detailed breakdowns of wedding budgets and how each couple pulled things off. Even if the wedding isn't in your area, it's helpful to know that an ultra-chic $3,000 wedding included a free venue, gifted photography, and a thrift store dress.

5.

Rethink "wedding." If you're planning a wedding for less than $10,000 (adjust that number for regional differences in wedding costs), the best thing you can do is reset your expectations around what a wedding should look like. A seated dinner in a fancy ballroom? Probably not going to work. But a family-style taco bar at your favorite park? Now we're talking! And creativity can extend beyond your venue. A morning wedding with a breakfast buffet and mimosas will set you back significantly less than a steak and potatoes dinner (and can be just as fun!).

6.

Set your priorities (and then stick to them). Sit down with your partner and make a list of your most important wedding priorities. That might include having as many guests as possible, serving the best food and drinks, or throwing an epic party. Then keep your eye on that prize. When you're having a minor meltdown later about the cost of flowers, ask yourself if having a *Pinterest*-worthy floral spread was one of your priorities. If it wasn't? Let it go. Find an affordable alternative or forget it altogether.

7.

Avoid the detail trap. It's easy to get distracted by all the wedding day details. Décor. Outfits. Pictures. But think about the weddings or events you've been to. Do you remember the centerpieces? The menus? The clever sign at the entrance? Probably not. What makes a great event is more ethereal than those things. It's about people, energy, and a moment in time. When you feel yourself getting stressed about the cost of centerpieces, remember that details are not what make a wedding memorable.

8.

Pick your battles. Parental expectations can be a major source of wedding planning stress. Remember that your parents and grandparents have probably been thinking about your wedding long before you even met your partner. While that doesn't mean they get a free pass, try to cut them some slack and pick your battles wisely. If something *really* matters to your family, and you only care about it a little bit, give them a win. But know when to hold firm: Protect your values, maintain your boundaries, and don't be a doormat.

9.

Don't make money assumptions. Outdated expectations around who will pay for your wedding don't take into account the reality of your or your parents' bank balances, so have a frank conversation with any invested parties. If asking for money is stressing you out, start with a lower-stakes question: "Do you have any expectations for our wedding?" You can then follow that up with, "Were you planning on contributing financially in any way?"

10.

Use your hobbies as inspiration. Feeling uninspired by the average wedding? Think about what you and your partner do in your spare time or on the weekends and then consider how you could incorporate that into your wedding. Are you beer and pizza people? Or are you more likely to be hitting up the local art gallery scene? Do you love arcades? Any or all of these can be the starting point for figuring out what you want your wedding to look and feel like.

11.

Cross it off before you start. Most online wedding checklists are filled with line items for weddings with six-figure budgets. And a *lot* of it is optional. If you sign up for an account somewhere like TheKnot.com, take advantage of the trashcan icon and delete anything that doesn't feel authentic to you and your partner. For example, are you planning on ordering invitations online? No? Then you don't need to meet with invitation designers first, so trash that item.

12.

Build your budget from your savings account. Trying to figure out how much wedding you can afford? Calculate your average monthly savings (or how much you can save if you're being frugal), then multiply that by the length of your engagement. Boom. You've got a rough idea of what you can personally afford to spend on your wedding.

13.

Budget your energy. Money is not the only finite resource in your budget. Your energy (physical and emotional) matters too, so make your energy budget as fixed as your financial one. Assign yourself one hundred energy points to spend throughout the planning process and use them wisely. Are you going to spend twenty hours researching venues? That's five energy points. Just like regular budgeting, you'll have to adjust your expectations when you run out of energy. And you'll be glad for it later.

14.

Don't start by cutting the guest list. Every piece of budget wedding advice under the sun will tell you to cut your guest list to save money. And it makes sense. Your costs go up as your guest list goes up. But only be ruthless with your guest list if you want to have a small(er) wedding. Or if you're inviting people out of obligation instead of joy. Otherwise, think about who you want at your wedding and plan a celebration you can afford around that number. It may mean getting creative with your catering or hosting it in a non-traditional venue, but the energy of your wedding will be dictated by who is partying with you, not the entrée.

15.

Do the math. It's common to look at the price tag for an all-inclusive venue or package wedding deal and think, "I could do that for way cheaper." And while you probably *can*, you want to do the *real* math before you make that call. Between renting furniture, hiring servers, and coordinating the logistics, an à la carte wedding can end up being more expensive (and that's not including time spent pulling it all together).

16.

Buy a wedding book and planner. You can find almost everything you'll need to know about wedding planning on the Internet, but sifting through search results to find relevant information can take forever. Physical wedding planners and books (like this one) take all that information and condense it into the most useful bits of advice, so pick up a few different books and read the highlights before going online. Also, if you're planning on a budget, look for words like "budget" or "practical" in the title to avoid resources intended for six-figure wedding budgets.

17.

Remember nothing is necessary. Absolutely *nothing* is necessary for a wedding except you, your partner, and a commitment. Everything else has been manufactured by our culture and the wedding industry. While throwing a formal party for 150 people is generally an expensive endeavor, a wedding does not have to be formal, or a party, or consist of 150 people. As soon as you start thinking your wedding won't be "real" without flowers or a seated meal, remember that none of those things will impact the end result: your marriage.

18.

Don't have a wedding you don't want. If in your heart of hearts you know you don't want to spend the time and money on a huge event, consider eloping. To the extent that it's appropriate within your culture and your relationship dynamics, let your family know if you're only having a big wedding to appease them. There may be a middle ground between a big wedding and an elopement—like a separate smaller ceremony or a reception your family plans where your only responsibility is to show up—that could make everyone happy.

19.

Reframe your spending. Even if you can afford your wedding, you may find yourself having a hard time reconciling spending so much on a single day of your life. One way to ease that anxiety? Shop small and support local artisans. Many wedding vendors are independent, woman-owned businesses, and most of your money goes directly to supporting the local economy of your wedding location. You can also shop your values by seeking out and supporting LGBTQ-owned businesses, BIPOC (Black, Indigenous, and People of Color)-owned businesses, and of course businesses owned by queer people of color.

20.

Have a short engagement. You can plan a wedding in any amount of time. Long engagements (a year or more) offer more vendor availability and allow ample time for guests to plan their travel, but long engagements can also lead to decision fatigue and wedding burnout. Short engagements (six months or less) mean working with what's available to you. You'll have fewer options, but sometimes that can be a blessing for your sanity. Short engagements can also save money via last-minute vendor deals. Only you can know which option is best for you and your partner.

21.

Your wedding is not your last chance to do things. The wedding industry will tell you that your wedding is your one shot to (fill-in-the-blank). But for the most part, that's not true. Your wedding is not your last opportunity to wear a fancy outfit, get your photos professionally taken, enjoy a beautiful bouquet of flowers, or whatever other upsell you're given. You can find or make opportunities to do those things in the future with your partner. Don't let a fear of future regret trick you into spending money on things you don't want.

22.

Forget about having a theme. If you want a themed wedding, by all means, have a themed wedding (a Harry Potter–style party sounds like a dream!), but don't get caught up in the idea that your wedding needs one (or that it needs "colors"). You can create a beautiful, cohesive event without tying it all together in a neat little bow. Think about how you experience someone's home. You want the décor to feel like it belongs to the same person, but it would be very strange to enter a house filled with the same two colors repeated over and over again.

23.

Create a burner email account just for your wedding. One of the easiest ways to save during wedding planning is to sign up for promotional emails from wedding brands (10 percent discount, here we come!), but the quickest way to regret that choice is by using your real email address. Create a new wedding-only account so that all your nuptial-related correspondence goes to one place. Just don't forget to check it!

24.

Let someone else build your checklist. You don't need to create your wedding to-do list from scratch. Sites like Zola.com, TheKnot.com, and APracticalWedding.com offer free digital wedding checklists that fill in the blanks for you. *Zola* also includes the option to add cultural or religious elements to your to-do list, like shopping for a broom to jump or getting your ketubah designed.

25.

Stay organized during wedding planning if you want a laid-back celebration. If you're Type-B and hoping to have a laid-back wedding, the best thing you can do is bring in help and bring it in early. If your budget allows for a planner or coordinator, that's your best bet, but even an organized friend who planned their own wedding can be a boon. The more organized you are while planning, the more relaxed you can be the day of. Plus, having backup plans for worst-case scenarios means you won't be stressed when things inevitably go awry on the big day, and can *actually* go with the flow.

26.

Tackle your to-do list from big to small. Your wedding priorities, budget, and big picture conversations should happen first, then figure out your guest list and venue. Once those are locked down you can move on to food, drink, and top priority vendors like catering and coordinating, then secondary vendors, and finally outfits, décor, and details. If you try to do it in reverse, you may end up with details that don't fit the rest of your wedding.

Twelve Ways to Make Your Wedding More Egalitarian

Incorporating tradition and connecting with your cultural heritage can be a meaningful way to start your marriage, but some wedding traditions are steeped in less-than-progressive history. If you're trying to imbue your wedding with more modern values, here are twelve creative ways to make it more egalitarian:

27. **Divide and conquer.** Early in the planning process, sit down with your partner, divide up tasks, and then figure out how to shoulder the burden equally. Maybe you split to-do list items by strengths and interests. Maybe one of you takes on research and the other tackles communication. Make your unofficial mantra "It takes two people to plan a wedding."

28. **Do your research!** If there's a ritual that's particularly important to you but is steeped in sexist tradition or excludes you due to your race, gender identity, body type, or sexual orientation, you can cut it or figure out if there's a way to modify it to be more modern and inclusive.

29. **Copy your partner on all wedding-related correspondence,** and ask your vendors that they do the same so that one person isn't the de facto contact person for your wedding.

30. **Forget gendered etiquette about who pays for the wedding** and instead have one-on-one conversations with family members about their desire to contribute to your wedding and their financial ability to do so.

31. **Have a gender-inclusive wedding party** and let people dress themselves, especially if you have queer or nonbinary people standing with you (and if you do have nonbinary folks standing up with you, don't forget to alert your vendors to their pronouns ahead of time).

32. **Walk the walk.** Signal to your guests that your wedding is an egalitarian affair by having both parents walk you down the aisle (and your partner's parents can do the same). Or walk yourselves down!

33. **Don't give anyone away.** You can replace that portion of the ceremony by inviting your community as a whole to state their support of your marriage.

34. **Change any language in your ceremony that feels outdated.** Have your officiant instruct, "You may now kiss," or announce you as, "Married for life."

35. **Everyone dances.** Make the honorary dances more egalitarian by including both of your parents and having your partner do the same. You can minimize the potential for added time by switching parents midway through a song.

36. **Switch up the toasts.** Wedding speeches are often given by men. Level the playing field and let other loved ones in your life give a toast.

37. **Make traditions less awkward.** If you're having a bouquet or garter toss, modify the tradition so that it doesn't single out unmarried people or make strangers engage in awkwardly intimate interactions. Or skip them altogether!

38. **What's in a name?** For a lasting impact, keep both of your last names or mutually change them.

39.

Start logistics early. You don't want to be hunting down guest addresses the day your invitations are supposed to go out. As you create your wedding to-do list, write down the easy-to-forget logistical details that need to happen early to avoid stress later. For example, if your wedding is in a different state, figure out the ideal time to be booking flights and mark that date on your calendar so you don't accidentally forget it in the midst of bigger wedding planning tasks.

40.

Ignore wedding style quizzes. When you sign up for an account on a wedding planning website, there's usually an accompanying "find your wedding style" quiz. But those quizzes are overly themed and limited to what's trending at the moment (e.g., beach bohemian or classical chic). While the quizzes themselves are harmless, those themes can unintentionally box you into searching for a specific style that may be inauthentic or hard to shop for. Skip the quiz and define your personal style for yourselves. You may find your ideal wedding is a combination of several styles.

41.

Think of wedding planning as marriage boot camp. Wedding planning isn't just about celebrating your relationship. It's a high-stress, high-cost, logistical maze that can put your relationship to the test. But that also means it's a great way to work out the kinks in your partnership that haven't been addressed yet (like navigating family expectations, getting your finances in order, etc.), so take your planning timeline as an opportunity to strengthen your bond and bring in whatever professionals you need to do that, from therapists to financial planners.

42.

Get premarital counseling. Weddings bring up a *lot* of baggage. Even if your relationship has a solid foundation, old family patterns have a way of resurfacing during big life events, so sign up for couples counseling early in the planning process. (Some religious practices even mandate it.) It can help you head off any unexpected drama while creating a healthy foundation for you and your partner in the future.

43.

Don't forget the prenup. Thinking about divorce when you're planning a wedding is decidedly unsexy, but it's also necessary if one of you has a trust, a business, or property. (If you're entering into marriage without any assets, a prenup may not be necessary.) Before you say "I do," sit down with your partner and have a conversation about how to protect yourselves if things don't work out. It can be a hard conversation but it's a necessary one.

44.

Don't wait if you need legal protections. Eloping before your wedding can be controversial (some people will think you cheated them out of seeing you get married), but if you need legal protections like health insurance or next of kin rights, you can always go to the courthouse and sign the legal paperwork now and save the ceremonial aspects of your marriage for your wedding. Disappointing some of your loved ones is a better outcome than spending wedding savings on hospital bills (and there's no rule that says you even have to tell anyone).

45.

Research real-world costs before budgeting. If you were buying a house, the first step you'd take would be to figure out the average cost of homes in your area. The same goes for wedding planning. Before figuring out your budget, research the real-world costs of services in your area. How much is the average florist? How expensive are the most popular venues? While those numbers might not impact the funds available to you, you'll walk away with a more realistic expectation of what you can afford.

46.

Earn miles as you plan. Get a credit card with airline points and put as many wedding-related expenses on it as you can to earn reward flights for your honeymoon travel. Most cards offer bonuses if you charge a certain amount in the first few months, and some have seasonal promotions that double or triple your miles. Just be responsible and only apply for a card you can pay off every month. Airline perks are not worth going into debt.

47.

Ignore standard percentages. When you're researching how to create a budget, you'll come across a lot of wedding percentage breakdowns that suggest you should devote a certain quantity of your budget to your venue, another percentage to your photographer, and on and on. The problem? Those percentages are based on industry averages that assume you have at least $25,000 to spend on your wedding. If you don't, then ignore those percentages altogether. You may find that you spend 50 percent of your budget on food, 25 percent on your outfit, and 0 percent on a venue because you ended up using a friend's backyard.

48.

Find loose change in your digital couch cushions. Apps like Qapital, Digit, and Acorns can automate your savings by helping you find extra cash in your budget. For example, you can set a rule to round up every purchase to the nearest dollar and deposit the spare change in your wedding account. While it might not add a significant amount of funds to your budget, these extra savings can be great for your "just in case" expenses.

49.

Save money with wedding classes. The wedding catch-22 goes like this: Professional wedding planners know how to stretch your dollar better than anyone else, but if you're planning a wedding on a tight budget, you probably can't afford to hire one. Online courses like *Choose Your Own Wedding* cost $40 to $50 per month (the equivalent of two pricey coffees per week) and you get a professional planner at your disposal, with insider insights at your fingertips.

50.

Track your budget in real time with an app. The estimated wedding budget line items you create at the beginning of planning are likely to evolve as you book your venue and hire vendors. Use an app like YNAB (You Need a Budget) to balance your wedding finances in real time as you make purchases throughout the planning process. The software is built to keep you and your partner accountable so that a couple of extra $500 expenses here and there don't turn into a $5,000 overage in your budget.

51.

Budget for "just in case" expenses. Unexpected wedding expenses will arise. That tent you thought you didn't need? Weather calls for rain. The bridesmaid who hasn't bought her plane ticket yet? She just lost her job. And the twelve projects you thought you would DIY? Well, some of those are going to be bought online. The "just in case" bucket is a fail-safe against surprises and mismanaged expectations. Add it now, avoid the hassle later.

52.

Community is the best hack. If you look at examples of big weddings for under $5,000 or $10,000, most of them have one thing in common: community (often in the form of gifted services, loaned party supplies, or cumulative DIY efforts). Before you start researching and planning for vendors and supplies, sit down with your partner and audit your network to figure out where you might have hidden resources. A free venue that isn't necessarily your first choice can free up the budget for vendors and perks you wouldn't be able to afford otherwise.

53.

Communicate roles clearly and early. Weddings may share certain characteristics, but expectations around roles and responsibilities of the parties involved will vary by region, religion, and the individual personalities of your loved ones. Have clear conversations early in the planning process to get any mismatched expectations out in the open. It's much better to manage disappointments early and proactively than by surprise six months down the line.

54.

Don't expect your family to change for your wedding. In an ideal world, weddings would encourage people to be their best selves. In reality, weddings have a way of turning up the volume on people's personalities. If your brother is normally flaky around important events, don't set yourself up for disappointment by giving him an important role in your celebration. The best thing is to accept that your family (and any associated feuds or drama) will be who they've always been and to manage your expectations early. And if you're preparing yourself for big disappointments, therapy is never a bad idea!

55.

Give family members special projects. Eager family members may want to help with the wedding, but sometimes their enthusiasm can be more anxiety-inducing than helpful. Try this trick: Give your loved ones a special project to own that they can execute independently. Just make sure it's one that you don't have a strong emotional investment in, in case their enthusiasm turns out to be short-lived.

56.

People only need to *think* they have input. As soon as you're engaged, people will want to tell you about the amazing wedding they went to where the couple got married on top of a hillside and anointed all the guests with rosewater (or what have you). Most of this advice will not be relevant to your wedding, but once you start in on what you *are* and *aren't* doing you open yourself up to even more unsolicited advice. A non-committal script like, "Oh, what a fun idea! We'll take it into consideration," is all you need to say to keep advice-givers happy.

57.

Know when to hold 'em. If you're making an unconventional choice about something like your cake, outfit, or first dance (anything that won't have an impact on your guests' good time but about which they are guaranteed to have an opinion), play dumb when asked about your plans. Say, "We're still working on that one," or, "We're hoping to finalize that soon, but you'll love it when you see it!" Just remember that this only applies to superficial details. If it might hurt someone's feelings (like if you're not inviting your uncle because he owes you money), let any involved parties know as soon as possible.

58.

Leave the country to cut your guest list. If you want to have a more intimate celebration but don't want to offend loved ones with a lack of an invite, consider a destination wedding. The cost of travel will (most likely) inhibit guests from attending, allowing you to have your cake and eat it too. But know your crowd. If your Uncle Jerry loves to visit the Bahamas every year, he is probably not going to be scared away by your Mexican resort wedding.

59.

Store spreadsheets and to-do lists in the cloud. If you're collaborating with multiple people to plan your wedding (or even just your partner), use Google Drive to create your working spreadsheets and to-do lists. (APracticalWedding.com has free Google spreadsheets you can download.) This ensures that you're always working off of a live copy and that any updates to the plan are reflected in real time. You can also use Google Drive to save your signed contracts (always download a PDF if you sign digitally), serving as an on-the-go planning binder.

60.

Get even more organized with Airtable. Google Drive and Microsoft Excel are both useful for spreadsheet data (to-do lists, guest addresses, day-of timeline) but they have limited functionality. Airtable mixes the spreadsheet functionality of Excel with the visual organization of *Pinterest*. You can save vendor contact cards, create interactive spreadsheets, upload documents, manage timelines, and even keep a calendar all for the same project. The connectivity cuts down on how many times you enter the same information, and it lets you share planning progress in a variety of different formats.

61.

Protect your privacy with a password. If you'd prefer to keep your wedding details private (from your boss, uninvited guests, or simply strangers on the Internet), make your wedding website password-protected or hide it from Google search. Password protection gives you the most security but is easier for people to lose and bug you about later. Hiding the website from Google means anyone with the URL can access it, but nosy people won't be able to find it by searching for your name. Check your wedding website provider to see what level of security they offer before signing up.

62.

Create a clever hashtag to organize your social posts. Hashtags are more than just the vanity plates of the Internet. They can be used to aggregate wedding photos and social media posts after the wedding is over (particularly useful if you're not hiring a professional wedding photographer). Not feeling creative? Use a hashtag generator like WeddingHashers.com to create one that no one else has.

How to Elope

If a wedding sounds like way more work than it's worth, there are several ways to get married that don't involve a big party. Eloping has come to mean many things—from two people at the courthouse to a handful of friends at your favorite park—but one thing's for certain: It's a lot less work. Here are ten things to keep in mind if your dream wedding involves nothing more than your partner and a few witnesses:

63. **Check the county clerk's website** before showing up at the courthouse. You may need an appointment to obtain a marriage license.

64. **Research wait times.** Some states allow you to get married on the same day that you pick up your license. Others require a wait of anywhere from twenty-four hours to several days in between. Short on time? If you have access to transportation, you can always get married in a nearby state where you don't live.

65. **Decide your level of formality.** You can elope and still hire an officiant, photographer, and florist and get decked out in your finest for an outdoor ceremony. You can also roll up to the courthouse in your favorite jeans or do something in between. Many a ball gown has been worn at the city clerk's office.

66. **Bring cash and your vital records.** You don't need much to get legally married but you will need vital records (driver's license, proof of divorce if you've been married before, and so on). And you'll need a way to pay for the marriage license. These requirements change by location, so do your research first.

67. **Prepare for hurt feelings.** If you exclude your loved ones from your elopement, be prepared for some folks to feel left out.

It doesn't mean you shouldn't do it, but don't elope with the expectation that they'll be happy about it. (And maybe tell your parents in advance to soften the blow.)

68. **Save money with an elopement photographer.** Elopements are smaller, shorter, and easier to shoot than traditional weddings, so most wedding photographers offer elopement packages at a significantly reduced rate. Search "elopement photographer" to find one in your area.

69. **Don't skip flowers if you want them.** If you have a few days' notice, you can order an elopement bouquet from FarmgirlFlowers .com and have it delivered to your house. For same-day flowers, pick up a bouquet from your local grocery store and wrap it with ribbon. (Some grocery stores will even arrange a custom bouquet if you call ahead.) You can find simple bouquet wrapping tutorials on *YouTube*.

70. **Make sure you have enough people in attendance** to make your marriage legal. Some states require one witness to legalize your marriage, others require two, and some don't require any at all. Pro tip: Your photographer can do double duty and serve as a witness.

71. **Bring rings and vows.** Your elopement doesn't need anything other than the legal minimum to get married (license, witness, and statement of intent), but rings and vows can help solemnify the occasion if you are hoping for a ritual with a little more weight.

72. **Send an elopement announcement.** You can help friends and family feel included in your marriage (or simply let them know it happened) with a post-wedding elopement announcement. Many online stationery companies have pre-designed templates just for the occasion. You just fill in the details.

73.

Save on flights with airfare deal alerts. If you want to get a jump on honeymoon planning (or even wedding-related travel), sign up for flight alerts from ScottsCheapFlights.com. Plug in your departure airport and the newsletter will send out alerts notifying you of any amazing travel deals leaving from that destination. *Scott's Cheap Flights* is particularly useful for last-minute international travel if you're willing to be a little flexible with your plans.

74.

Get a custom URL. There are tons of free wedding website providers that let you create a quick landing page for your event with RSVP, registry, and wedding location details for your guests (*Zola* and *Minted*, to name a few). If given the option, create a custom URL that's easy for your guests to remember. Your name plus your partner's name is a good place to start if it's not already taken. Avoid any clever puns or homophones that might get lost in translation. (Save those for your wedding hashtag.)

75.

Create a color story with online color palette generators. Not everyone is into aesthetics. If pulling together a cohesive color palette for your wedding feels out of your wheelhouse, use Canva to do it for you. Upload a reference photo or select a color from the app and Canva will generate a bunch of complementary colors that are guaranteed to look good together. Use those suggestions as a guiding force for your décor.

76.

Save time with Gmail templates. Emailing a few dozen venues and vendors to get pricing information takes time. Avoid having to create a brand-new email from scratch each time (or digging through your sent email archives) by utilizing Gmail's template feature. You can save a handful of different scripts ahead of time then auto-populate the body of your email when it's time to contact someone new.

77.

You can't avoid a "dated" wedding. Weddings are built on traditions (even if you're throwing most of them out the window), and they are always going to reflect the decade in which you got married. Lean into it. If you plan your wedding around what you're less likely to hate in ten years, as opposed to what makes you happy right now, you're going to end up with something in the middle that you only half-like.

78.

Track your time and energy. Saving money usually means investing more time, either through extended research or DIY. To avoid overextending yourself, use an app like Toggl to keep track of how your hours are being spent. When you notice the stress mounting, you'll know why and can adjust accordingly. For example, it might be time to abandon that DIY project you thought would take two hours but has actually taken ten.

79.

Don't compete with professional designers. When you're looking at real weddings for inspiration, take note of the couples' occupations. Professional designers, artists, and wedding vendors are often able to pull off weddings more affordably due to the skills and resources—like software, printers, and DIY supplies—they've acquired on the job. If you're not in a creative field, it's unfair to set yourself up with the expectation that your DIY or design skills should match the people who do this kind of thing professionally.

80.

Beware the fake wedding. You'll find plenty of examples of beautiful tablescapes or wedding décor on *Pinterest* and *Instagram*, but if you can't verify that the inspiration comes from an actual wedding, proceed with caution. Styled shoots may look like real events but they are often not replicable at scale. What's affordable for one table can quickly become astronomically expensive when you multiply that number by fifteen or twenty.

81.

Get comfortable with phone calls. If you hope to plan your wedding the way you might do anything else online (with readily available prices and a "buy now" button), you'll find yourself quickly disappointed. The wedding industry is not always modernized, so while it may take extra time and effort, phone calls, emails, and in-person visits are the only ways to get tactical information. Just limit your outreach to avoid burnout and have canned responses ready for when the information you get isn't what you were hoping for.

82.

Give yourself a phone script. Most venues and vendors don't list their prices online, so call a few of your top choices and use this script to get a sense of their average cost: "Hi, I'm researching to see what kind of (venue/vendor) we can afford for our upcoming wedding. We don't have a date yet and aren't looking to schedule any in-person visits at this time, but can you give us a general idea of what most of your clients spend for a wedding with (insert number of guests here) or can you email us a price list?" Most should be able to send you a PDF of their services.

83.

Use the rule of three. Wedding research can get exhausting. Avoid decision fatigue by narrowing your top venue or vendor contenders down to three. (If you're unsure of pricing, you can up this number to five or six to ensure you find options within your budget.) Once you've found three options you like, stop your search and reach out to them to get a sense of pricing and availability. This way your inbox won't be overwhelmed with responses and you won't be overwhelmed by choice.

84.

Done is better than perfect (make this your mantra). If you're lucky, a handful of your wedding choices are going to be exactly what you hoped for. In reality, most of what you end up with is going to be a combination of what you like and what you can afford. When you've found a venue, vendor, outfit, and so on that works, stop researching immediately. If you interview a wedding photographer and love them, hire them on the spot. There's no need to do extra work if your gut tells you you're making a good choice. Done is better than perfect.

85.

Open a separate bank account just for the wedding. When surprise wedding costs creep up on you it will be tempting to dip into your personal savings to cover them. If you're committed to staying on a budget, open a separate bank account just for your wedding funds, complete with its own dedicated debit card. It's harder to overspend when you have finite resources in the bank.

86.

Don't spend cash gifts before you get them. Cash gifts are not uncommon, especially if you are a fairly established couple and you opt for a more limited registry. However, you can't guarantee that your guests will write checks instead of giving off-registry gifts, so don't count your wedding cash as part of your budget until it's physically in hand. Spending money you don't have yet is just another way of going into wedding debt.

87.

Budget your wedding album into your cost estimates. Wedding albums usually fall under the "after the wedding" budget umbrella but it's hard to convince yourself to spend more money once the party's over, so include a wedding album in your budget before you start planning. It doesn't have to be expensive. You can get high-quality lay flat albums from online shops like *Shutterfly*, ArtifactUprising.com, MilkBooks.com, and more for a few hundred dollars (and remember to use those 40 percent off coupons whenever you can!).

88.

Tacky is in the eye of the beholder. Weddings are an amalgamation of ritual, culture, and tradition. When those things collide, opinions tend to be strong. You and your partner will likely experience judgment from strangers and loved ones about your wedding (no matter how careful your choices), but remember: "Tacky" is subjective. As long as you and your partner are being gracious and thoughtful hosts, a plastic tablecloth or digital invitation isn't actually going to ruin anyone's day.

89.

Create alternatives for traditions that don't resonate. If a particular wedding tradition doesn't fit your values, ditch the activity but keep the vibe. For example, if you don't love the idea of a cake cutting, invite your guests to hit a piñata instead. Or, if you want the energy of a bouquet toss in a format that's kid-friendly, change it to a candy toss. Think about what the tradition is trying to do, then rework it in a way that matches your values.

90.

Use your wedding to honor your culture. The wedding industry is always looking for the next big trend, which makes it rife with cultural appropriation (aka, when you use decorative elements, customs, or rituals from a culture you don't belong to because they seem cool). Cultural appropriation can be hurtful (you wouldn't want someone to take something of yours just because they liked it or thought it was pretty), so it's best to avoid what doesn't belong to you. Instead of looking outward, consider which aspects of your own culture you can incorporate or thoughtfully modify, or create something completely from scratch. The easiest way to know if a tradition is appropriative is to do the research. Most online searches can give you that answer in about five seconds flat.

91.

Have a spontaneous small wedding. If you're having a small enough wedding (usually ten people or fewer), you can skip the venue rental costs and get married almost anywhere as long as you're not being obtrusive (think your favorite museum, Grand Central Station, a local garden, etc.). If the location is owned by a small business, get permission from the owners before you show up. Otherwise be spontaneous and hope for the best.

92.

Merge traditions with help from the pros. If you're marrying someone from a different faith, you'll have two different sets of religious rules to keep in mind when planning your wedding. But the Internet can help! While most American wedding advice is centered around Christian wedding traditions, websites like 18Doors.org can assist you with navigating the unique challenges of merging Jewish and Christian wedding traditions and finding clergy who are versed in interfaith weddings. And MPVUSA.org offers global resources for Muslim and Christian interfaith weddings and marriages, including *Facebook* groups where you can connect with other interfaith couples.

93.

Don't force yourself to have a dance party. If dancing is not what you and your partner consider a good time, think outside the box for your reception venue and associated activities. You can have an intimate dinner party heavy on conversation, host a picnic and provide lawn games to keep your guests entertained, or serve brunch with a mimosa bar. There are plenty of ways for your guests to have a good time that don't involve cutting loose on the dance floor.

94.

Plan a pop-up wedding (with help). Pop-up wedding planners like PopWed.co and PopTheKnot.com offer all-inclusive small wedding packages that include a venue, officiant, and photographer for roughly $2,000 to $4,500. Pop-up weddings usually have a maximum guest count of fifteen to thirty-five guests and typically don't include a reception, but you can always take your nearest and dearest out for a tasty lunch or dinner afterward and call it a day. It's like a mini wedding with none of the work.

95.

Plan for the marriage. Planning a wedding means planning for everything that comes after. If you don't know where to start on the big conversations (especially regarding finances), MeetYMO.com (*Yours, Mine & Ours*) has guided classes that can help you figure out how to start a discussion and where to go next. They'll also connect you with professional lawyers, financial advisors, and therapists. The website was started by divorce attorneys and their goal is to make sure you don't end up in their office.

96.

Get your affairs in order. No one wants to talk about worst-case scenarios, but coming up with an end-of-life plan now is one way to protect your partner later. If you haven't drafted your wills or discussed healthcare directives, now is the time. JoinCake.com is a free service that guides you through end-of-life planning, identifying next of kin, and creating wills, and you can store all your essential documents within the platform. (Pro tip: Don't put this one off until after the wedding.)

CHAPTER 2

Shopping for Venues and Hiring Vendors

97.

Go all-inclusive. Destination weddings sound luxurious. Beachside entertainment? Open bar? Must cost six figures. But destination resorts make most of their money on lodging, so their all-inclusive weddings are usually packed with lots of free perks to entice you to spend a week there. And the best part? Your honeymoon is built in. Just remember that a destination wedding can impact your RSVP rate, so if travel is cost prohibitive for your guests, the savings might not be worth it.

98.

Dig for a diamond in the rough. Really cool venues can cost thousands of dollars just for the use of a raw space (we're talking an empty building that *you* have to fill), but that doesn't mean you can't find an off-the-beaten-path venue that's still affordable. Peerspace.com is like *Airbnb* for venues, aggregating interesting raw spaces that you can rent by the hour. Most of them aren't traditional wedding venues but they come with much more affordable price tags. *Airbnb* and *Craigslist* can also turn up unique venues at affordable rates if you're willing to hunt a little.

99.

Don't ignore history. Many large venues (particularly in the American South) were once slave plantations and, as a result, the sites of mass brutality. In addition to your own moral reasons for wanting to avoid these sites, many wedding vendors will no longer work plantation weddings as a matter of principle. Before booking your wedding at a historic mansion, research the history and make sure your venue checks out so that you don't end up feeling regretful of your choices or embarrassed by your wedding photos in the future.

100.

Check your surroundings. If you're queer or a member of a marginalized group, it's not always easy to tell if a rural venue (and its surrounding areas) is going to be welcoming. Before you book a tour, check the venue's website to see if they've worked with couples who look like you in the past.

101.

Don't fight city hall. Marble staircases and ornate columns: Does it make you think *government building*? It should. But city halls aren't just for elopements and marriage certificates. Some cities boast beautiful historic buildings where you can get married (in some cases with as many as one hundred guests) for as little as a few hundred dollars. If you want to rent out the whole building, the price is often still more affordable than what you'll find at a traditional venue.

102.

Raw spaces aren't necessarily money savers. Outdoor spaces with low price tags can be very tempting when you're working with a smaller budget, but an empty space means you have to calculate the cost of everything into your estimate. This may mean your caterers need to bring a portable kitchen (which could add costs or limit your menu) or that you need to bring in fancy porta-potties to make sure your guests have a place to pee during the festivities. In the end, the venue with the lowest starting price may end up being more expensive than the all-inclusive venue that sent you into sticker shock in the first place.

103.

Check the venue restrictions before finalizing your vision.
Does your venue allow tents on the lawn? Can you light candles inside?
Before signing on the dotted line, make sure that any fine print fits
within the logistics of your wedding. If you can only accommodate a
seated dinner by putting guests outside and tents aren't allowed, what
does your rain plan look like?

104.

Look for the weekend warriors. Wedding vendors typically fall
into two categories: full-time pros and weekend warriors. Vendors with
day jobs (aka, weekend warriors) don't always have as much experience
as full-time pros, but the benefit is they often offer much more affordable
rates. If you find a vendor whose prices seem like a mismatch for their
skills, it may be that they simply don't use their business as their primary
means of income. Just be mindful that a vendor with a day job may have
a slower email response time and fewer business protections in the event
that something goes wrong.

105.

Blogs can score you 10 to 20 percent off vendor prices. The easiest way to find a wedding photography discount or a deal on other service-based vendors is to follow wedding accounts on *Instagram* and scout wedding blogs for sponsored posts. When wedding vendors promote their businesses, they often include discounts that range anywhere from a free engagement session to 10 to 20 percent off your total booking. These deals are usually limited time offers, so browse often and be ready to book when you find the right one.

106.

Use *The Venue Report* to get venue estimates online. Venues are notorious for withholding pricing information on their websites (though sometimes you can find a service menu buried as a PDF in the site's navigation). For quick estimates, use *The Venue Report* or download the Wedding Spot app. When you create an account, you get immediate access to venue listings with minimum and maximum rental fees, plus all the amenity information you need at a quick glance. Just remember that estimates aren't hard costs, so follow it up with a phone call or email to see if there are any hidden fees.

107.

Get married in the off-season. If you're competing with other couples for a popular wedding date your choices and price options are going to be more limited. Consider booking off-season. What that means will vary by your geography. In the southwest, off-peak probably looks like summertime, and in New England you'll likely save more money with a winter wedding. In general, October is quickly becoming the most popular month to get married. Take note!

108.

Use your wedding to shop your values. A big portion of your wedding budget will go directly into the pockets of small business owners. While you don't want to reduce your hiring choices to a checklist, be mindful of who you're including on your vendor team and support communities you care about. Work with an LGBTQ-owned catering company. Choose a venue that prioritizes accessibility for people with disabilities. Seek out BIPOC wedding professionals. Weddings are a $70 billion industry and your hiring decisions help decide what that industry looks like today and in the future. Plus, the experience and skills of a diverse team can bring added value and insight to your day.

109.

Go on a date with your vendors before hiring them. Your baker or alterations professional doesn't necessarily need to be your next BFF. What matters is that you like their work and they have basic customer service skills. But, when you hire a photographer or coordinator, you are signing up for someone to be with you from start to finish during your wedding (plus several months of communication beforehand). In addition to checking their portfolio for inclusivity and matching values, make sure you feel safe and comfortable with your vendors in person *before* signing that contract. A bad personality fit can be a major buzzkill during an otherwise joyful day.

110.

Look for included amenities. A cool venue might have an affordable baseline price but once you start adding in extras like furniture rentals, lighting, sound equipment, and staffing, the price could easily double. Keep your eye out for venues with included amenities (tables, linens, an onsite wedding coordinator) to save on costs. And don't knock the all-inclusive venue! The wedding factory where your cousin got married might not be as hip as that downtown loft but all-inclusive means everything is covered.

111.

Take a photo tour of your venue. Many wedding venue websites are outdated or lacking in real wedding content. If you want to see what a venue looks like on the inside without having to visit, look for photographer blogs. Professional wedding photographers often optimize their blog posts with keywords to help you find their work. Google the venue name with your city and state to find search results that showcase real weddings photographed by professionals. It's the armchair way to get an instant read on how your wedding might look and feel.

112.

Nonprofits aren't in it for the money. One of the easiest ways to save money on a venue is to look for a nonprofit organization that doubles as a venue space (think museums, gardens, historical societies, etc.). Since nonprofit buildings are often public spaces, there isn't much need for décor and the rental fees are almost always lower than your average for-profit wedding venue. HereComesTheGuide.com lets you filter venues by price and type so you can quickly find an affordable nonprofit venue in your area.

113.

Think TGIF when choosing a wedding date. Wedding venues and vendors don't typically offer discounts if there's a chance they can get their full rate (and there are only so many Saturdays in a year). An easy way to save money? Get married on an off day like Friday or Sunday. And if you really want to save, get married on a weekday. Just remember that a weekday wedding might impact attendance, especially if you have a lot of out-of-town guests.

114.

Don't get married in a church just because it's pretty. If you don't belong to a church but want to get married in one, check the guidelines (or speak with a leader within the congregation) before inquiring about having your ceremony there. Houses of worship usually have rules around weddings and may require that you be a member of the church (or at least a practicing member of their religion) before utilizing the building.

115.

Las Vegas isn't just for elopements. If you hate the idea of a stuffy wedding and still want to have a good time, Vegas has tons of options for affordable ceremonies. A few hundred dollars will take care of a venue, flowers, limo, and photography, and the quality ranges from stereotypical Vegas chapels all the way up to classy casinos. You can elope with just a few of your nearest and dearest or host a 150-person ceremony and let the nightlife be your reception.

116.

Avoid DIY catering (unless you really love cooking). There are plenty of ways to hack traditional catering (ordering from a restaurant, for example), but cooking your own food should be a last resort. While it can be done, catering is time-consuming and labor-intensive and requires a lot of planning and attention to food safety. Only sign yourself up for that kind of commitment if it's because you really, really want to and you know what you're doing.

117.

Max capacity means minimizing your guests' space. Shopping for a venue can be a guessing game. How many people will RSVP yes and how many people can the venue hold? While you might be tempted to max out your venue's capacity, doing so may sacrifice your guests' comfort (aka, packing them in like sardines). If you want more space to move around comfortably, aim for a headcount that's 10 to 20 percent below the venue's stated limit.

118.

Remember the season when booking venues. If you're planning your wedding far enough in advance, you may be doing venue tours in a different season than when you'll be getting married. A church that's comfortable at the end of October may be sweltering hot in the middle of July if there's no air conditioning. Jot down seasonality questions before taking a tour and make sure your prospective venue has the amenities you'll need.

119.

Check for bathrooms, kitchens, and electricity in non-traditional venues. When you're shopping around for venues, look for the crucial amenities. If your venue doesn't have adequate restrooms (or is on a delicate septic system), a large kitchen, or has difficult-to-reach and limited electricity, you may be signing yourself up for additional costs in the form of porta-potties and generators down the line.

120.

Check local event calendars before booking a venue. If you're getting married in a smaller community where hotels might be limited, reference local event calendars before committing to a date. While your venue might be available, if your wedding date is the same weekend as the big festival in town your guests might have a hard time finding an affordable place to stay (or any place at all), and local street traffic may add a logistical headache that you probably won't want to deal with.

Ten Non-Traditional Wedding Venues That Bring Their Own Décor

Non-traditional wedding venues are often one of the first things couples look at when trying to figure out how to cut costs. While they aren't always money savers (always do the math!), these venues offer a unique backdrop that means you won't have to worry about décor:

121. **Restaurant:** Restaurants are great all-inclusive venue options. They already have all the furniture and décor you need, plus built-in catering. And if dancing isn't your vibe, a dinner party wedding in a restaurant can take the pressure off.

122. **Backyard:** If the weather is going to be nice, find a big backyard, pull up some food trucks, and host a casual party on the lawn. Just remember you'll have to rent furniture (and possibly a tent and fancy porta-potties).

123. **Campground:** Invite your guests to spend the weekend hanging out by the campfire, swimming in the lake, and bonding over s'mores. Bonus: You can have your rehearsal, reception, and post-wedding festivities in one place.

124. **Brewery or beer garden:** If you and your partner are proud beer snobs, a brewery can pay homage to your favorite pastime with an industrial vibe and lots of beer garden–style seating.

125. **Public park:** Public-owned venues usually come with really affordable price tags (and your money goes toward supporting your community). Check with the venue to see if you'll need any extra permits or if there are limitations on what you can do in the space.

126. **School:** Schools are usually closed on weekends. Ask if you can rent out any of the large gathering spaces (field, playground, cafeteria, gymnasium), then kick it prom style.

127. **Historic site:** Historic sites have impeccable architecture and décor so you won't have to DIY a thing. They may have stricter rules about what you can and can't do in order to protect the site, so ask about open flames, alcohol restrictions, and noise limits.

128. **Art gallery:** For an ultra-cool vibe, check your local art galleries to see if they rent their spaces for private parties. Just make sure you know what exhibit will be showing at the time of your event. (A retrospective on violence in America isn't exactly wedding-friendly.)

129. **Rooftop:** Do you (or someone you know) live in an apartment with a view? You may be able to rent the rooftop for your ceremony and host a cocktail-style reception.

130. **Music venue or theater:** Music venues are already set up for a rockin' dance party, so make it your own. There may not be a kitchen available, so look at food trucks or alternative catering options for dinner plans.

131.

Research your local municipal rules. Municipal codes vary from town to town, and especially if you're planning on getting married in a quiet touristy area that has ordinances to prevent rowdiness, they may be stricter than what you'd expect. Want to have a bonfire at the beach after your wedding? You may need a permit. Planning on partying until the wee hours of the morning? Double-check quiet times. Start this research early so you have plenty of time to file paperwork and make requests for exceptions as needed.

132.

Remember to give people room to move. If you're setting up your own reception space, be sure to measure your dining layout with the chairs pulled out. Leave enough room for people to get up from their seat during dinner without having to disturb the guests behind them. Otherwise, you may be trapping your guests in the wedding equivalent of a window seat on an airplane.

133.

Do a lighting check. If photography is a high priority for your wedding (and there's no rule that says it has to be), think about the time of day you're getting married and how much light will be available in your venue. A gothic church might have major romantic vibes, but if it's pitch black during the ceremony and your photographer can't use a flash you may need to hire someone who specializes in low-light capability.

134.

Consider liability insurance for a non-traditional wedding. Hidden gem venues and raw spaces don't always have their own insurance policies for large events, so protect yourself with a policy that covers you in case something goes wrong. (You can get a lot of coverage for a few hundred dollars.) MarkelInsurance.com, ProtectMyWedding.com, TheEventHelper.com, Wedsure.com, and WedSafe.com are all trusted carriers. Read the fine print of each policy to see if the coverage matches your needs and the unforeseen circumstances most likely to impact your wedding (e.g., extreme weather).

135.

An open bar is not a requirement (no matter what anyone says). Hosting a big party means taking care of your guests: feeding them, entertaining them to an extent, and possibly providing booze. However, that doesn't mean you need to give them a one-way ticket to an alcohol free-for-all. If your budget prohibits an open bar, a wine and beer reception or a few signature cocktails is plenty to keep everyone in good spirits. And if you can't or don't want to have alcohol at all? You can still have a banging good time.

136.

Party in daylight hours to manage guest expectations. If you're worried that people might be scandalized by your lack of an open bar, change up your party schedule. Daytime events make it easier to get away with light or no alcohol at all. Not sure how to make it work? Think mimosa bar, mint juleps on the lawn, or white sangria with a few beer options.

137.

Think outside the steak. Blame the sad chicken and overpriced steak of 1980s weddings for the pressure you might be feeling to feed your guests a gourmet meal at your wedding. But if you're trying to cut your budget, food and drink are the most effective line items to revisit. Pasta, pizza, barbecue, and buffets can all be filling and feel fancy while accommodating several dietary needs. Better yet? They don't demand a huge price tag. In fact, your guests probably won't even notice they weren't served a "wedding meal."

138.

Serve luxury menu items as appetizers. If you have your heart set on serving a local specialty (Maryland crab cakes, Maine lobster, California tri-tip) but can't afford to feed your 150 guests a Michelin-rated meal, miniaturize your menu and turn your entrées into appetizers. Change crab cakes into crab balls. Make your lobster roll a fried lobster ravioli. Or pass out tri-tip crostini in place of sandwiches.

139.

Order from your favorite restaurant. DIY wedding food doesn't have to mean a potluck reception or cooking your own dinner. You can semi-DIY by ordering self-service catering from your favorite restaurant. Barbecue and Mexican restaurants are usually experienced with catering to large groups so a wedding won't be out of their wheelhouse. Add an à la carte bartending service to handle drinks and you'll never have to spend a moment sweating in a kitchen.

140.

Look outside the mainstream. If you're not part of a white, heterosexual couple, the wedding industry can feel like it wasn't made for you, but if you look beyond mainstream wedding media you'll find inclusive outlets producing content for a diversity of couples (and almost all of those websites have vendor guides). While not an exhaustive list, for couples of color, start with MunaLuchiBridal.com, BlackBride.com, and NuBride .com (or in print, *Our Love in Color* and *The B Collective* magazines). For LGBTQ+ weddings there's EquallyWed.com, BlackGayWeddings.com, and HAndHWeddings.com. For Jewish weddings, SmashingTheGlass.com. And for a mix of everything, APracticalWedding.com and CatalystWedCo .com specialize in sharing weddings from a variety of different backgrounds.

141.

Add taxes and service charges to your catering estimates.
When reviewing catering or venue estimates, always scan the document
for additional fees before you fall in love. There's usually a 20 to 30 percent tax and service charge that is not factored into the baseline price
that can dramatically increase your invoice total. And always check the
fine print about what is or isn't included: Linens, staff, setup, and breakdown might all be extra.

142.

Search styled shoots for vendor links. Wedding inspiration on
Instagram and *Pinterest* isn't just there to make you feel inadequate. Every
single real wedding or styled shoot has a team of actual wedding professionals who brought it to life. Go to your favorite wedding blog and
search for your city and state, then scour the vendor credits at the bottom of those features. You'll find a bevy of artists along with direct links
to their portfolios. You can even do the same for venues.

143.

Follow the hashtags. If you're looking for vendors who have worked in specific environments (say, a big Indian wedding or someone who has experience with trans couples), use *Instagram* hashtags to find them. A vendor who uses a hashtag like #transwedding or #desiwedding is generally trying to advertise the kinds of clients they like working with. While they might not be geographically close, they may be willing to travel or have a network of vendors that serves your area. Follow the rabbit hole.

144.

Look outside your zip code to find affordable vendors. Local vendors are always more affordable, right? Not always. If you're planning a wedding in a more remote location, or just a place without a ton of wedding talent, you might be stuck choosing from the handful of local vendors who live in that zip code. But many photographers, planners, and coordinators have low or no domestic travel fees (and if you're close to state lines you may even be within their existing travel policy), so expand the borders of your search and you might find a better deal.

145.

Start with your own connections to get better deals. While you may be tempted to ask your favorite vendor for a deal on their services, friends and family-style discounts are easier to come by, so start within your own network. You may be surprised to find that your uncle's former math student is a budding florist and wants to pay it forward for that time he helped her pass calculus, or your best friend's intern is starting a photography business and needs to build a portfolio.

146.

Ask an ally to reach out to vendors for you. When you're queer, reaching out to vendors means coming out over and over again, not knowing if you're going to face rejection from someone you've never met, so recruit an ally to do it for you. Ask a trusted friend or wedding party member to field responses from potential vendors so they can filter out any potentially hurtful correspondence.

147.

No price doesn't mean more expensive. Wedding vendors often omit prices from their websites for fear of scaring away potential clients (the flip side of sticker shock), but lack of pricing doesn't mean your prospective vendor is prohibitively expensive. A quick email will get you a price list, and you may find that what you thought was a high-end vendor is actually well within your budget.

148.

Consider a barter instead of a discount. Looking for a discount on wedding services? Instead of asking for a reduced cost, consider whether there might be a barter you can offer if you or your partner specialize in a trade. For example, if you're a lawyer, can you review a wedding coordinator's contract in exchange for a reduced rate? Or if you're a carpenter, can you offer a custom piece in exchange for a few extra hours of your photographer's time? Just remember to treat trades like cash and make sure expectations are covered under your contract (with deadlines and dollar values assigned to everything).

149.

You won't get something for nothing. It's tempting to reach out to your favorite vendors to ask if they'll be willing to give you a discount on their services but most wedding professionals won't simply cut their fees without a tradeoff. When phrasing your ask, be sure to include something that makes it worth *their* while as well (fewer hours, for example). You're much more likely to get a deal that way.

150.

Ask for freebies in the name of inclusivity. Asking for free wedding services is generally impolite (vendors have bills to pay too), but when it comes to diversity and inclusion it's okay to break the rules. If you find vendors who claim to be allies but their portfolios don't contain anyone who looks like you, reach out and ask if they'd be willing to offer one free trial before you book. That way you can see if a prospective hairstylist understands updos for 4C hair or if a prospective photographer can pose two nonbinary people for engagement photos without reverting to gender stereotypes. Proceed with caution, though. The emotional energy involved in being someone's learning opportunity might not be worth it in the end.

151.

Wedding coordinators often pay for themselves in savings. It's tempting to think you can run your own wedding show if you've been planning it this whole time (who knows it better than you?), but you can't enjoy your wedding if you're also your own vendor. While a professional wedding coordinator may seem cost prohibitive, the discounts they're able to secure and the money they can help you save often make up the difference, especially if you're going to be using rental companies where they might have a discount.

152.

Trade day-of services with another couple. You can't be emotionally present at your wedding if you're also serving as your own day-of coordinator, but not everyone can afford a professional wedding planner or coordinator. If you know a very organized person who is getting married near your wedding date (or even just in the same year), offer to trade day-of coordinating services. You keep them organized on their wedding day and they can keep you in check on yours.

153.

Reach into vendor networks for recommendations. The most talented wedding vendors aren't always the ones who are great at marketing, which means if you don't live in a major metropolitan area it can be hard to find independent vendors (DJs, makeup artists, florists). If you're hitting a wall and you've already lined up other vendors like a photographer or coordinator, ask them for recommendations. Their friends and colleagues will probably share a vibe not unlike the one that drew you to them in the first place.

154.

You don't have to settle for micro-aggressions. If a prospective vendor's website is chock-full of "bride" and "groom" language or doesn't feature any couples of color, there may be other implicit biases lurking beneath the surface. You don't have to settle. Whether you're queer or part of a marginalized group, or simply want to work with vendors who prioritize inclusivity, you can hold vendors to a higher standard than the status quo. If you're getting married in an area where the options are more limited, you can always reach out and encourage vendors to change problematic wording, then make hiring decisions based on their response.

155.

Always review your contracts. Your wedding might be the first time you have to deal with contract negotiations. Don't let that scare you. Contracts are there to protect you and your vendors from unforeseen circumstances. (Every professional you hire should have one. If they don't, that's a red flag.) Then, check your contracts for potential issues. Does your venue only allow an hour for setup and breakdown? Does your photography package not include digital negatives? Those are things you want to know *before* you write a big ol' check. And don't be afraid to negotiate for better terms. The worst anyone can say is no.

156.

Friendors need contracts too. Things can go wrong, even between friends (sometimes *especially* between friends). If you're hiring a friend to help with your wedding, aka a friendor, they need a contract too. If your friend is a wedding pro by trade, ask for their standard contract. If they are a hobbyist, you can download a simple contract online for free and modify it to your needs. Contracts don't need to be fancy; they just need to be clear. What is your friend doing, when are they doing it, and how are they being compensated?

157.

Hope for the best but assume the worst in your contracts.
When negotiating your contract, always assume the worst-case scenario.
What would happen if your photographer simply didn't show up on
the day of? What would happen if your venue suffered an unexpected
structural issue right before your wedding? That isn't to say any of those
things are *going* to happen, but the job of your contract is to have a clear
game plan if they do.

158.

Compensate your friends to make favors more official. It's easy
to flake on a favor. If someone has agreed to do your wedding for free, find
a way to make it more formal. Contracts help, but a little bit of compensa-
tion (even if it's far below their normal rate) can help formalize a freebie in
the eyes of your friendor. And consider planning a backup option in case
your favor gets abandoned for a better-paying gig. (It happens.)

How to Self-Cater Your Wedding

Catering your own wedding is not an endeavor to be taken lightly, but it can be done with a lot of organization and teamwork. If you're considering it, here are ten things to keep in mind so that everyone goes home well-fed:

159. Stick with semi-DIY. Self-catering doesn't have to be an all-or-nothing deal. Can you order a main course from your favorite restaurant but provide passed appetizers that you've cooked yourself? Or maybe you save on dessert by baking a bunch of pies. Taking on a smaller piece of the puzzle will be a much more manageable task.

160. Find reliable help. You can't actually self-cater your wedding and enjoy it at the same time, so recruit a lot of help early in the process and make sure they're fully committed (this is not the time for flaky friends). Then follow up with clear and specific instructions.

161. Consider a potluck dinner. To avoid taking on the burden of self-catering entirely, invite your community to participate in a potluck dinner. However, don't leave your menu to chance. Calculate your needs and make specific requests of people so you don't end up with twelve entrées and no sides.

162. Aim for simple and filling. The path to self-catering success is through recipes you know well that cook easily. Think about simple crowd-pleasers that can be cooked in large batches using simple tools (like slow cookers or casserole dishes), and test your recipes first before cooking a hundred servings.

163. **Raid the frozen food aisle.** You can find plenty of delicious heat-and-serve appetizers and prepared ingredients in the frozen food aisle of most grocery stores. Trader Joe's makes particularly tasty frozen appetizers. Add a fancy cocktail napkin and you've got yourself an hors d'oeuvre.

164. **Heat-and-serve.** There's a big difference between serving home-cooked food at your wedding and actually *cooking* the day of (you want the former). Aim for freezer-friendly dishes that can be prepared ahead of time and reheated just before they're served.

165. **Don't overlook a cold dish.** Charcuterie plates, fruit baskets, cheese boards, and other cold dishes are filling and easy to outsource to the novices in your help network. Use them liberally.

166. **Mind your food safety.** It goes without saying that you don't want to end up with a bunch of sick guests at your wedding. Practice safe handling, keep an eye on temperatures, and avoid using ingredients that spoil quickly.

167. **Remember the servingware.** Every dish you serve will need a platter and a set of serving utensils. Gather these early and don't leave home without them or you'll end up with a bunch of food and no way to get it onto guests' plates.

168. **Do it as a last resort or a labor of love.** Unlike other DIY projects, self-catering isn't something you can do halfway. Don't take the responsibility lightly. If there are other budget catering options available (like self-service catering, a pizza truck, or a taco bar), really consider if the additional time and effort is worth the money saved.

169.

Friends can't be guests and vendors at the same time. Before accepting an offer of help, first ask yourself: Do I want this person to be able to enjoy themselves at our party? Invitations, baking, crafting, and beauty services are all great opportunities for loved ones to help with the wedding, but catering, photography, and coordinating are all-day commitments. Your loved ones will likely be too busy to have a good time.

170.

Hire student artists as vendors. If you're comfortable with a trainee, look into music, art, or cosmetology schools for vendors like ceremony musicians, photographers, and hair and makeup artists. Students are usually enthusiastic about earning a few hundred dollars for a few hours spent doing the thing they love most. And you might be surprised at the professional-quality talent you find. Just be sure to properly vet them if you're hiring for a role you care about and, as with all vendors, sign a contract.

171.

Hire a photographer for portraits only. If you really want a professional wedding photographer but can't afford full-day coverage, consider hiring someone for portraits only. This works best if you're getting married outside of the busy season, on a weekday, or on short notice and the photographer wouldn't be sacrificing a full day's pay to cover your event. Another tip: You can always dress up in your wedding finery for a weekday portrait session *after* the wedding. Someone who charges thousands of dollars for a wedding will usually only charge a few hundred dollars for a weekday session.

172.

Cross-reference multiple websites for accurate vendor reviews. Most vendors include testimonials on their website, but you'll find more honest client feedback by cross-referencing those testimonials with reviews on sites like *WeddingWire*, *Yelp*, and *Google*. Consistent reviews across multiple platforms should mean a consistent quality of work from your vendor. And don't be afraid to ask about any negative reviews. How your vendor responds to that kind of query can say a lot about what it's like to work with them.

173.

Rent equipment to get better results. Hobbyists don't usually have state-of-the-art equipment, so if you're hiring amateur vendors or friendors for your wedding, consider renting upgraded equipment where it would make a difference. Better speakers for a DJ or nicer lenses for a photographer will directly impact the quality of their services at your wedding (and the prices for rentals are often more affordable than you'd think).

174.

Don't hire people you don't like (even if you love their work). What if you find an incredible artist to photograph your wedding but you don't like his personality? Do. Not. Hire. Him. It doesn't matter if the photos could be published in the pages of *Vogue* alongside an editorial spread by Annie Leibovitz—if you don't like his personality, your discomfort will show up in every one of your pictures.

175.

Ask prospective photographers to see a full wedding gallery.
Most wedding photographers will show you a highlight reel of their best
work on their website or portfolio, but your wedding won't be all pic-
turesque backdrops and perfect lighting. Ask potential photographers
if you can see a full wedding gallery from start to finish (ideally in an
environment similar to your venue) to get a sense of how they handle
less than ideal shooting conditions.

176.

Ask amateur photographers to shoot and deliver RAW. Most
professional wedding photographers will give you edited digital negatives of your images and not the RAW files, which are unedited and
can't be viewed without special software. If you're working with an amateur, make sure they are shooting RAW in addition to JPEG and ask
for the original files alongside the edited images. While you likely won't
need them, RAW files can make up for a myriad of issues if your amateur photographer misses the mark with lighting, exposure, or editing.

177.

Book an up-and-coming photographer. Wedding photographers charge more as their skills improve (more experienced photographers know how to handle more situations, thus ensuring your photos turn out great regardless of the environment), but if you book far enough in advance you'll be hiring someone for their future talent at their current prices, so look for promising up-and-comers. They'll get lots of additional practice before your wedding and their skill level should be markedly increased when it's your turn.

178.

Don't waste your hair or makeup trial. If you're working with a professional hair or makeup artist, they'll usually include a free trial with your booking. (And if they didn't, ask if they can.) If you've booked an engagement session with your photographer, schedule your hair and makeup trial for the same day and you'll have professional makeup for your photos. Bonus: Stretch that look even further by taking yourselves out to a fancy dinner afterward.

179.

Take engagement photos inside. If your wedding photographer includes an engagement session, skip the trip to an unfamiliar neighborhood and choose locations that are meaningful to you, like your home or your favorite restaurant or bar. You'll be more at ease and you'll have a visual time capsule of where you lived when you got engaged. (Plus, if you take pictures in your own living room, you can BYOB.)

180.

Head to your local club store for floral supplies. For DIY flowers, club stores like Costco and Sam's Club sell bulk floral supplies at affordable prices that you can order in advance (and many couples note that the quality is way better than you'd expect). Not up for DIY? Those club stores also sell pre-arranged wedding collections that include bouquets, boutonnieres, and centerpieces starting at $250.

181.

Let someone else do the design for you with semi-DIY flowers.
If you love the look of modern wedding flowers but don't live in an area
with a lot of creative florists (or can't afford the prices of the hip floral
studios), online boutiques like Bloominous.com and FlowerMoxie.com
deliver semi-DIY floral packages that include everything you need to
assemble *Instagram*-worthy bouquets and centerpieces for a price that
falls between DIY and buy (around $120 for a bridal bouquet, $50 for a
small centerpiece, and $10 for a boutonniere).

182.

Hire a Tasker for setup or breakdown. If you're DIYing your
wedding, consider hiring local help from TaskRabbit.com for setup and
breakdown. You'll pay up to a few hundred dollars for the extra help,
but the cost is significantly less than hiring a professional wedding coordinator. Plus, you'll have the added bonus of saving your wedding party
from having to hang decorations while they're trying to get ready.

183.

Do your own makeup touch-ups. If you're getting your makeup professionally done and are worried that it might come off during the festivities, you can always ask your makeup artist for a quote on touch-ups. If that quote proves cost-prohibitive, ask if you can buy the lipstick they used and do touch-ups yourself. (They might even be willing to gift it to you.) Professional foundation and eye makeup should last the evening and you'll be able to handle lips on your own.

184.

Get a friend to officiate your wedding. Want to save a few hundred dollars and have a super-personalized ceremony? Ask a friend or loved one to be your officiant. While there's no rule that says the person who performs your ceremony has to be the one who legally marries you, it's really simple to obtain the right to legally officiate ceremonies. Use the site GetOrdained.org for an almost instant online ordination (handy to have in the event of last-minute officiant needs!) plus guidelines on how to perform a wedding ceremony.

185.

Beware the closed hotel block. Hotel room blocks are one way to ensure your out-of-town guests will have somewhere to stay (and they usually come with a solid 10 to 20 percent or better discount for your guests), but not all blocks are created equal. Open or courtesy blocks won't hold you responsible for unbooked rooms (they'll just release them to the public) but closed blocks make you foot the bill if the block is left underbooked. Check your contract carefully before agreeing to pay fees for open rooms.

186.

Rent your flowers. From a few feet away, silk flowers look almost identical to the real thing. You can save up to 50 percent off the cost of fresh flowers by renting pre-designed silk floral arrangements from SomethingBorrowedBlooms.com. A big bouquet will set you back $65 while a centerpiece (vase included) is just $28. There are a variety of styles to choose from (classic, colorful, romantic), and when you're done, simply send them all back.

187.

Choose in-season flowers. Seasonality can wildly impact the cost of your arrangements. To keep costs down, stick with flowers that are in season and locally grown. While you can easily find a seasonal flower chart online (ProFlowers.com has one that's also organized by price), the best person to ask is your florist. Give them a general idea of your style, then ask which flowers will be in season at the time of your wedding. But be ready to compromise: If you have your heart set on something distinct like peonies, there might not be an affordable or in-season equivalent and you'll need to adjust your expectations accordingly.

188.

Sign up for hotel rewards to get free rooms. If you're getting married in a hotel owned by a chain, sign up for their rewards program. The cost of your reception means you may be able to rack up points quickly and cash them in for free rooms to use during your wedding or when planning your honeymoon.

189.

Defer savings by purchasing gift cards during promotional periods. Wedding planning timelines and online sales don't always line up perfectly. If you see a sale and aren't ready to buy, what do you do? If you're shopping for wedding invitations on Minted.com, for example, you can purchase a gift card with a discount code and use it later, saving 25 to 35 percent off your wedding paper.

190.

An overstaffed bar is better than an understaffed one. You want to aim for one bartender for every seventy-five guests if you're hosting a beer and wine reception or one bartender for every fifty guests if it's a full open bar. Err on the side of excess. Waiting in line for a drink is a quick recipe for cranky guests, so if you're on the fence and can afford it, it's better to have too many bartenders than too few.

CHAPTER 3

Inviting Guests and Asking for Gifts

191.

There's no such thing as the perfect wedding date. Cross-reference your date with any VIP guests to avoid conflicts, but you can't ensure everyone will be able to make it, no matter how hard you try. One thing to remember: Scheduling your wedding on a holiday is a blessing and a curse. Holidays mean time off, which makes it easier for guests to say yes, but they may also have alternate plans. If you're planning a wedding for a holiday weekend, let your guests know as early as possible and remember that airline ticket prices may be higher.

192.

Calculate your time per guest. Figuring out a guest list estimate can be a stab in the dark, but one place to start is with your time per guest. The average seated wedding reception is four hours. Subtract thirty minutes from that for eating and bathroom trips, then divide that number of minutes by how many guests you're inviting. Boom. That's about how much time you'll get with each individual guest. Now get real with yourself about how you want to experience your wedding. Intimate and one-on-one or a packed party? Both are equally valid.

193.

Create your ideal guest list before getting realistic. It's easy to get into the weeds with your guest list. If you invite this person, does that mean you have to invite these other three people? Take the pressure off early. Put together a guest list that isn't based in any kind of reality. Who would you invite if money and capacity were no issue and you could say yes to all your parents' plus-ones? Once you have *that* list, identify the parameters that might help you whittle it down (people you haven't seen in five years, coworkers you don't hang out with socially, etc.).

194.

Cut your guest list by asking one simple question. When you're trying to whittle down your guest list, creating rules can help. (Have you and your partner both seen this person in the last five years? Are they a regular at your holiday festivities?) One simple way to decide whether someone should get an invite is this: Ask yourselves, if this person were the only guest to show up at our wedding, would we still want them there? Your answer is an immediate and honest gut check on who should make the cut.

195.

Skip the obligation invitations. When thinking of who to cut from your guest list, consider the emotional value of your invite and the real-world repercussions of cutting them. If you invite your mom's BFF from college, will she genuinely have a better time at the wedding? Probably, yes. If you don't invite your boss, are they *really* missing out? If you aren't getting a demotion because of it, then pass. And remember, just because someone invited you to their wedding does not mean you owe them an invitation in return. Hurt feelings and family feuds notwithstanding, guilt and obligation are terrible reasons to have someone at your wedding.

196.

Know the RSVP rates in advance. You'll be surprised by who ends up coming to your wedding and who sends their regrets (it's never the people you think!), but before you commit to your venue or start putting postage stamps on your paper suite, know the average RSVP rates so you can make a smart estimate of your total guest list. For local guests, assume a rate of about 90 percent Yes and 10 percent No. For out of towners, the Yeses shrink to about 70 percent.

197.

Create a backup guest list. Prepare for the possibility of surprise regrets in advance by creating an A guest list and a B guest list. The A list is all your must-have attendees who receive the first round of invitations. As accepts and regrets roll in you can send out your B list invites if space allows. Having your backup guest list at the ready gives your guests the most amount of time to consider and RSVP to your wedding, thus increasing the chances that they'll actually come.

198.

Accommodate the abilities of your guests. When putting together your guest list, make a mental note of whether any of your guests might require accommodations to properly experience your wedding. For example, if you're inviting a guest who is deaf, consider hiring a translator for your ceremony (your guest may even have someone they already work with). Or, if you're planning on having a mostly standing ceremony, allocate a handful of chairs to elderly relatives, pregnant people, and anyone whose body doesn't tolerate standing for long periods. If the purpose of your wedding is rallying your community around your partnership, you'll want everyone to be able to participate equally.

199.

Calculate invitation numbers by household. When calculating your invitation needs, remember to calculate by household, not the total number of guests. If you're inviting 150 people but most of them are couples or families, your invitation order will probably be closer to seventy-five or one hundred. On the flip side, always include a couple of backup invitations with your order in the event of envelope mishaps or last-minute guest list changes.

200.

Give plus-ones when you can. How do you pick who gets to bring a significant other? Some etiquette says all significant others get an invite (with emphasis on "significant"). Others say only live-in significant others make the cut. If you're on the fence, think about your guest's experience. Will they know anyone else at the wedding? Clever matchmaking via seating arrangements can't erase the awkwardness of being at a party when you don't know anyone else. If you can afford the extra plate, do your guests a solid and let them bring a plus-one. On the other hand, if you're inviting a group of people who all know each other and you're iffy on the plus-one, feel free to skip it.

201.

Infants can break the "no kids" rule. Many wedding receptions are now adult-only to cut down the head count, but consider the age of the children on your guest list. While parents of school-age children may have an easy time leaving their little ones with a sitter, parents of infants may have a harder time leaving their babies at home (for a variety of emotional and logistical reasons, like having to find a place to pump at your wedding). It's generally accepted that the "no kids" rule can be overlooked for newborns and infants.

202.

Send save the dates to maximize attendance. Save the dates are not a required piece of wedding stationery, but they can help your guests prepare for your wedding long before you send out your actual invitations. If you have a lot of out-of-town guests and you want to maximize the chances that they'll be able to attend, send out a save the date as soon as you know your wedding date and location. Unlike invitations, there's no "too early" for save the date cards.

203.

Let technology nag people for their addresses. Wedding websites have long offered RSVP tools (and thank goodness for that!), and in addition to collecting attendance information they can also aid in getting your guest list organized. If you're trying to track down guests' mailing addresses, your wedding website might have a built-in feature that can help. Just send an address request to your guests using the website and it'll automatically import the response data into your guest list spreadsheet. It makes invitation addressing and RSVP tracking much easier down the line.

204.

Be clear about who's invited. Traditional wedding etiquette says that only the guests whose names are on the invitation are considered invited to the event, but sometimes that gets murky. Does an invite addressed to The Johnsons include their two school-age children? The mother-in-law who lives with them but isn't related to you? If you want to be extra clear, you can indicate the number of spaces that have been reserved for them on your RSVP card. For example, an invite addressed to The Johnson Family that says "Four seats have been reserved in your honor" makes it clear that the mother-in-law isn't invited.

205.

Save on invitations with a seal-and-send invite. The more pieces of paper you include with your invitations, the pricier they're going to get. If you like the look of luxe stationery, you can save money with a seal-and-send invite. (Minted.com and BasicInvite.com both have seal-and-send options.) These folded invitations include your wedding details and a perforated RSVP card that can be removed and mailed back to you. They don't even need an envelope because the address is printed right on the back.

206.

Lose the RSVP card. Thanks to the Internet, you no longer need a separate card with your invitation to explain where the wedding will take place and how to get there, but what about the RSVP card? While it can be nice to have for older guests, most of your wedding attendees will be Internet-savvy enough to figure out how to type in your wedding website URL and RSVP yes or no (and if they aren't, they probably know someone who is), so skip the RSVP card and print your wedding website right on your invite.

101

207.

Use Google to unlock special stationery discounts. You can expect to pay anywhere from $1.50 to $5 per wedding invitation with most online invitation shops, though the cost goes down the more you buy. For invitations under $1 each, your best bets are AnnsBridalBargains.com, Vistaprint.com, Zazzle.com, *Canva*, and Walmart.com. Not seeing the right price? Google "wedding invitations under $1" and the resulting links may reveal promotional pricing or discounts.

208.

Use a $20 laminator for DIY custom foil. You can get foil or letterpress invitations from most online shops for less than $3 per invitation, but if you want to save some cash, make larger foil décor, or get creative with colors, a simple laminating machine (you can buy them at most office supply stores) and some heat-reactive foil sheets will get you started. All you need is a black and white laser-printed design (the laser printing is key; an inkjet printer won't work), run that through the laminator with your foil, then peel it apart. Voilà! The foil will stick to anything that was laser printed and your design is now metallic.

209.

Get semi-custom invitations for off-the-rack prices. Online invitations are still created by real designers. If you order from an online shop like Minted.com, you may be able to utilize design services to personalize your invites for a semi-custom look. This can range from $5 for a designer to help with the layout to $100 or more for completely custom designs.

210.

Hack a DIY invite with a printable design. If you're not a designer, customizing wedding invitations can be a lot of work, but you can cut your costs and effort way down by purchasing a PDF invitation design from an independent seller on *Etsy* and then having it printed at your local print shop, Staples, FedEx, or even at home on your own printer with some nice card stock. Just be mindful not to get too fancy as super thick paper can jam printers and cost you more money later (110-pound weight card stock should be safe).

Wedding Invitation Dos and Don'ts

You may have heard that your wedding invitation sets the tone for your celebration. While that's true to an extent (though don't let it convince you that you need more expensive stationery), the primary purpose of your invitation is to convey information. Here's what to keep in mind as you put yours together:

211. **Do** include a clear indication of precisely who is invited to the wedding on the outside of your envelopes.

212. **Don't** let people talk you out of digital invitations if that's what you really want. They can be affordable, beautiful, and effective. Companies like Greenvelope.com even send them by text so they aren't in danger of getting lost in someone's spam folder.

213. **Do** triple-check that you've spelled your wedding website URL correctly on your invitations.

214. **Don't** spring for the full invitation suite if you don't want it. It's not necessary to include a direction card or reception card if the major details of your wedding are clearly indicated on the invitation (who, what, where, and when).

215. **Do** include an address for your venue in case there are multiple locations in town with the same or a similar name (it happens!).

216. **Don't** put your registry info on the invite itself. (It's an etiquette rule that's still in play.) Include your wedding website URL and link to the registry on there.

217. **Do** give a deadline and method for RSVPs so you don't end up having to hunt down late responders (or at least not as many).

218. **Don't** expect everyone to send their RSVPs back before the deadline (i.e., build extra space into your timeline for latecomers).

219. **Do** invite people even if you know they can't come. The gesture is often a meaningful one, and sometimes plans change!

220. **Don't** skip the stamp on your RSVP envelope if you're including paper response cards. It's an extra cost out of your pocket but it increases the likelihood you'll get them back.

221.

Get high-end design details for cheap with a DIY invitation kit. If you're looking for fancy invitation styles like laser cutouts or foil but don't want to pay $2 or more for your invites, buy an invitation kit online. These pre-designed kits include everything you need to create fifty invitations for $20 to $50, and all you have to do is print your wedding details on them. They can be found on *Amazon*, LCIPaper.com, or Walmart.com. You can also Google "invitation kit" for more options.

222.

Use Canva to get free wedding invitation designs. You don't need Photoshop to design and customize your own wedding invitations. While Photoshop offers more controls, it also requires a fair amount of learning to get the hang of it. The design software Canva, on the other hand, has free wedding invitation templates that you can personalize without any prior design experience and then print directly from the *Canva* website for about fifty cents per card.

223.

Ask for reprints if you find an error. Word-of-mouth referrals are a driving force in the wedding industry, so businesses usually prioritize strong customer service in order to keep reviews positive. As a result, many online stationery companies will offer a reprint for free or for a reasonable fee if you accidentally mistype something on your wedding invitations. And honestly? As long as the logistical information is correct, typos aren't the end of the world. Just fix it on your website.

224.

Don't resend invites if you misprint your website URL. Most invitation mistakes can be rectified on your wedding website, but if you accidentally write the *wrong* website address on your invitations, you don't need to send out a whole new set. Just check if the misprinted URL is available, then forward it to the correct website address so your guests can find the information they need.

225.

Use wrapping paper to hack an envelope liner. If you're a stationery-lover, envelope liners are a fun, big-impact wedding invitation detail (though they definitely fall under the "only if you really want to" category since envelopes are the first thing to get thrown away when you receive an invite). You can easily hack an expensive-looking envelope liner using wrapping paper and an envelope liner template. Print out a free template on MarthaStewart.com or order a kit from PaperSource .com, then cut out your paper and use glue sticks or a glue runner to adhere the liners to your envelopes.

226.

Trade envelope liners for colorful envelopes. Invitation details are only worth the effort if you really care about paper because most of it goes right into the recycling bin upon opening, but if you want to add a little flair to your stationery, opt for a colorful envelope. They're less time-consuming than envelope liners (you can buy them as an add-on from places like Minted.com or BasicInvite.com) and it'll only set you back an extra $15 to $25 per one hundred invitations.

227.

Get cheaper postage by sending a postcard. Postage can take an otherwise affordable wedding invitation and turn it into an expensive endeavor (odd sizes, shapes, and weights are things to look out for), but the easiest way to save money on your stationery costs is to send out a postcard for things like your save the date or RSVP cards. Postcard stamps cost only thirty-five cents compared to regular stamps at fifty-five cents.

228.

If you can print it out, you can make it a sign. For day-of wedding stationery, save money by converting printed information into a sign. For example, if you're serving a buffet-style meal, there's no need for a menu on every plate. One large menu sign and labels on the buffet table will get the message across. One caveat: If your ceremony involves reciting specific words, or has cultural elements your guests might not understand, printed programs are often worth the expense.

229.

Send out invitations midweek. The faster your invitations get opened and responded to, the easier it is for you to make decisions that rely on a head count. If you send out paper invitations on a Wednesday, they're more likely to arrive on the weekend when your guests have the time and energy to engage with them (but modify accordingly by geography or if you know your mail takes a little longer).

230.

Create a free wedding monogram for easy DIY details. Minted.com's free monogram maker lets you input your wedding details and then download a semi-customized monogram that can be printed onto sticker paper or turned into a rubber stamp. You can use your monogram for any personalized wedding accoutrements like favor bags or welcome packets or as a logo for your wedding website.

231.

Save paper and postage with digital invites. Paperless save the dates and invitations are an economical and eco-friendly way to send out your invites and collect RSVPs. You can find beautiful free templates at Evite .com and PaperlessPost.com. (If you want the experience of "opening" an envelope, they also have premium designs.) And if you're worried about a few elderly or technology-averse guests, you can always send out a small handful of supplemental paper invites (*Paperless Post* even has a partnership with Paper Source so your digital and paper invites can match).

232.

Ask someone else to review your invitations for you. It's easy to miss simple errors when you've spent a dozen hours going over the details of your invites. After you've reviewed them for accuracy, ask a detail-oriented friend to check twice for typos, missing information, and other errors. And if you accidentally get something wrong anyway? Rectify it on your wedding website.

233.

Avoid hand cramps with free pre-addressed envelopes. Hand addressing your wedding invitations seems like a good way to save money in theory. In practice? Say hello to your newly developed carpal tunnel syndrome. It's also totally unnecessary. Most online wedding invitation companies now offer free recipient address printing on envelopes (and you can select from a handful of designs for extra personalization), so unless you have a recently acquired calligraphy hobby and want to practice your form, let technology take care of this one for you.

234.

Don't set yourself up to lick a hundred envelopes. Have you seen the episode of *Seinfeld* where George's fiancée dies from licking too many wedding envelopes? While that *probably* won't happen to you, moistening one hundred envelopes with your tongue is still not the best use of your saliva. Instead, opt for a glue stick, embossed stickers, or a pre-moistened sponge to seal your envelopes. (Stickers and glue have the bonus of being less likely to come apart in the mail.)

235.

Use a hot glue gun to hack a wax seal. Fancy invitations are not a wedding requirement but they can be fun (especially if paper is your love language). If you love the look of a wax seal but are concerned about melting wax with an open flame, you can purchase glue gun–compatible wax sticks that work with all standard wax seals. The total cost to seal one hundred invites is around $25.

236.

Check postage costs before ordering nonstandard invitation sizes. If you fall in love with or choose to make a cool invitation that isn't a standard correspondence size or is particularly heavy, check the postage requirements before you commit. Seemingly innocuous details (like square cards) can cost extra. Added postage costs will set you back anywhere from an additional fifteen to thirty-five cents per envelope, which can add up quickly (or result in a bunch of return-to-senders if you accidentally send out your invitations without enough postage).

237.

Label your RSVP cards to avoid confusion about who they are from. Mailed RSVPs seem like they would be hard to screw up—all your guests have to do is fill in the blanks with their names and choose an entrée—but many an RSVP card has been returned blank with only a yes/no reply. Avoid having to track down absentminded guests by numbering the back of your RSVP cards and assigning each number to a guest on your list. Then, when RSVP card #8 comes back with a "happily accepts," you'll know it's from Great Aunt Millie.

238.

Give yourself a buffer for late RSVPs. You'll want to send out your wedding invitations about eight to twelve weeks before your wedding and set an RSVP date that's three to four weeks before the big day. That should leave plenty of time to follow up with any AWOL guests who reply late without feeling like you're in crunch mode (or getting too close to your catering confirmation deadline).

239.

Adjust the RSVP date for your B list. If you end up having extra room to include guests from your B list, keep in mind the RSVP date on your wedding invitations. Since B list invites typically go out after you've received the bulk of your replies, you may end up accidentally sending out an invitation with a reply-by date that's already passed.

240.

Keep private events off the wedding website. Your wedding website should be a hub for all of your wedding's logistical details, but be careful that the information you're sharing isn't going to cause any hurt feelings. If you're hosting invite-only events (such as a rehearsal dinner), keep those off the website or host them on a password-protected page where only the invited guests know the URL. This also prevents well-meaning attendees from accidentally thinking your invite-only event is open to the public.

Ten Registry Ideas That Won't Clutter Your Home

If you and your partner have been living together and don't need extra kitchenware or home goods, it can be a challenge to figure out what to put on your registry. Universal registries give you more control over your gifts, allowing you to ask for experiences and subscriptions. Here are ten registry ideas that won't clutter your closets:

241. **Food and wine gifts.** Give yourself a date night in with a subscription to a beer of the month club or a fancy cheese platter from your favorite local creamery. Live near a winery? Add a membership so you can keep enjoying your gift year-round.

242. **Books.** Yes, technically books are physical gifts, but they probably won't take up extra space on your kitchen counter. Register for new cookbooks, specialty editions of your favorite titles, or, if you're very committed to going clutter-free, gift cards to your favorite digital library or audiobook subscriptions.

243. **Streaming services.** Are you and your partner entertainment hounds? Add streaming services to your registry. (Some universal registries like *Zola* already have them built in.)

244. **Magazine or newspaper subscriptions.** The best gifts are the ones that keep giving (or showing up in your mailbox once a week or month). Add your favorite newspaper, magazine, or monthly literary subscription.

245. **Wedding album credits.** Once all the wedding money is spent it can be hard to justify additional cash funds for a wedding album.

Add a credit for your favorite album company and let your wedding guests buy your album for you. (*Artifact Uprising* gift cards are already part of some universal registries and the company makes gorgeous wedding albums.)

246. **Honeymoon activities.** While you can create a separate honeymoon registry with sites like HoneyFund.com, you also can hack your universal registry by setting up separate cash funds specifically for the activities you want to do on your honeymoon (e.g., one cash fund for a cigar tasting and another for a catamaran trip).

247. ***Airbnb* gift cards.** If you and your partner travel frequently, add travel-related items like gift cards for *Airbnb* or your preferred airline to your registry. Depending on where you register, you can add gift cards like this with the click of a button.

248. **Date night excursions.** Looking for a way to keep things adventurous after the wedding? You can register for unique couples experiences on sites like VEBOLife.com or with a *Zola* registry. Choose anything from cooking classes to skydiving passes to a spa day for two.

249. **Plants and gardening supplies.** If you're a plant person, you know there's no such thing as too much greenery. Online nurseries like Bloomscape.com let you add statement foliage to your home with potted plants. Or, if you have outdoor space, register for gardening tools and live plants and you'll have a hobby waiting for you after the honeymoon.

250. **Activity kits for two.** When you want to have a date night in, simply reach for a pre-assembled activity kit. You can choose from a variety of hobby kits, from brewing your own kombucha to making your own cheese. Thursday nights will never be boring again.

251.

Tell your guests if there isn't going to be an open bar. Thanks to cultural norms (and movies), most people know what to expect when they show up at a wedding, but if you're doing anything that might be unexpected and impacts how your guests should prepare, let them know as soon as possible. This is especially true if they'll need to bring cash or a debit card to the event. Your wedding website is the perfect place to put this information. Remember: You don't owe anyone an apology for your choices, but you do owe them a heads-up!

252.

Don't dictate a dress code. It's always kind to let your guests know the formality of your event along with any extenuating circumstances they'll want to consider as they pick their outfits (like your venue's mile-long hike to the ceremony location), but being a good host means letting your guests be the adults they are. Give information, but don't tell people what to do. And avoid anything veering into overly rigid dress code territory, like asking your guests to all wear the same color. That only works for the Kardashians.

253.

Test drive Google Maps before committing your driving directions to paper. If you're including an insert card with driving directions to your venue (or even if it's just going on your website), do a test drive first to make sure there's nothing that could accidentally get your guests turned around. Sometimes even a pinpoint accurate GPS can send you to the wrong parking lot and you don't want your guests driving in circles when your ceremony is about to start.

254.

Let guests know about religious requirements. Does your ceremony take place in a religious venue with a dress code? Don't assume your guests will know what's appropriate (especially if you have guests attending who are not religious or who were raised outside of your faith or culture). Your website is an ideal place to say "Our venue requires that shoulders be covered during the ceremony, so please bring a sweater or jacket if you plan on wearing a sleeveless or strapless dress," or whatever may be appropriate.

255.

Ask queer guests what would make them most comfortable.
If you have queer and gender nonconforming guests coming to your wedding, ask in advance if there's anything that would make them feel supported among mixed company. For example, would it be helpful to offer pronoun pins at the reception, or would that make them feel more singled out than supported? It's always better to ask than assume. Don't forget to consider your seating arrangements too and keep more close-minded guests at a distance.

256.

Consider budget when booking room blocks. If you're planning on having a lot of out-of-town guests, room blocks allow people to book discounted rooms from hotels that you've pre-vetted (and can be helpful if you want to encourage them to stay at the same location). If you want to increase the chances that your guests will use your room blocks, consider offering a few different hotel options with varying price points (luxury, mid-range, and budget).

257.

Go beyond the big-box registry. If you and your partner already cohabitate, you may have all the housewares you need. While it's important to remember that a wedding gift is something freely given (and never required), you can still steer your guests in the direction of what you want with a universal registry. Modern iterations of the universal gift registry go way beyond physical products, allowing you to add experiences, subscriptions, honeymoon activities, or cash funds to your wish list.

258.

Minimize your registry to maximize cash. If you have your heart set on cash gifts, encourage your guests to write checks by putting together a very small registry filled with gifts from a traditional retailer. The handful of housewares will satisfy the staunch traditionalists in your network and leave room for your extended family to spread the word that you're mostly hoping for financial support. When your guests see that all your gift options have been fulfilled, they'll have to shop off-registry or give cash. Just be prepared for the few guests who will take your lack of registry items as an opportunity to buy you a weird piece of ceramic art.

259.

Turn on group gifting. Figuring out the right balance of items on your registry can be tough. Is it ever okay to ask for a big-ticket item like a piece of furniture? (Answer: Know your crowd.) One way to soften the ask is to turn on group gifting. Depending on the registry platform you use, this can be as easy as clicking "make it a group gift" when adding an item to your registry. This allows your guests to contribute smaller amounts to more expensive items without having to deal with the annoying logistics of *actually* splitting a gift.

260.

Use a travel registry to ask for honeymoon experiences. Sometimes older guests have a hard time getting on board with cash registries, preferring to give something more tangible. If you're saving up for your honeymoon, travel registries allow you to register for specific honeymoon-related experiences. Your guests can help you pay for a couple's massage, a culinary class, an adventurous excursion, or any other travel-related activity you can imagine. While some travel registries let your guests buy travel experiences directly, others use an honor system and the gift itself is equivalent to cash. The latter can come in handy if you think your travel plans might change and you don't want to lock yourself into a location-specific activity.

261.

Place your most wanted registry gifts at the top and bottom of your registry. Due to the way people read websites, the most commonly purchased registry gifts are the ones featured at the top and bottom of the page, so stack your most desired items accordingly. (The top right-hand corner is another hot spot.) You can also utilize the "most wanted" features on modern registries like *Zola* to highlight the products you're really excited to get.

262.

Rearrange your registry order if you're having gift guilt. If your registry allows you to customize the order of your gifts, put less expensive items before higher priced ones. People often make judgments about the content of a web page based on the first thing they see. Your registry will read as less posh if more expensive registry items come after a handful of more affordable gifts.

263.

Don't register for what you can't store. When you're building a registry online, it's easy to forget that the gifts you're going to receive are physical objects that take up space. Make a plan for where all your new stuff will go after the wedding. Do you have space on your counter to store a stand mixer? Will a full set of china fit in your spare cupboard? If you don't have room, don't put it on the list.

264.

Register for who you are, not who you hope to be. You can use your registry to kick off traditions you look forward to in your life as a married person (e.g., registering for formal china if you plan to host your family's Thanksgiving dinner), but be realistic about what that looks like for you. If you've never baked a cake or pie in your life, you probably won't want a giant stand mixer taking up space on your counter. But if you live for your morning cup of coffee, by all means ask for the super cool espresso maker with all the features. The best way to know the difference is to ask which gifts are an extension of how you already live your life (just maybe leveled up a bit) and which are an extension of your *Instagram* fantasy.

265.

Send out thank-you cards in real time. Etiquette says you have a year to send out thank-you notes for wedding gifts, but waiting to send them all at once just creates more work for you later, leaving room for you to accidentally forget what your cousin sent you. Send out thank-you cards as gifts arrive. It'll make the job smaller and you'll thank yourself later.

266.

Buy now, ship later. Wedding gifts have the unfortunate habit of arriving whenever they feel like it, but between DIY projects and your regular household maintenance, you might not have room for any of them just yet. So, take advantage of shipping delays. Some registries (like *Zola*) will let you delay shipment of your gifts so that you don't receive packages before you're ready for them. Additionally, *Zola* lets you return gifts for store credit before they even arrive, so if you change your mind about that mixer, you can turn that unwanted gift into something you actually need.

267.

Use your completion offer to get a major discount. Registries want you to end up with everything you asked for (it's the only way they make money), so most of them have a built-in completion offer. That means if you didn't get everything you need and you want to buy any remaining registry items yourself, you get an automatic one-time 20 percent discount (give or take) to make it happen. Most completion offers are one-time use, so consolidate your purchases to take advantage of your discounts and be mindful of any expiration dates.

268.

Think outside the kitchen. Unless you and your partner are professional (or even amateur) chefs, you probably don't spend the majority of your home life inside your kitchen, so think outside the bread box. Do you and your partner go camping every summer? Maybe now is the time to upgrade your tent. Do you love music? Add a record player or a nice set of speakers to your registry. Older or more traditional guests may scoff at the idea of registering for electronics, but younger friends will likely jump at the opportunity to purchase a gift that reflects your interests.

269.

Go for double or nothing on household goods that wear out fast. If you're registering for commonly used household items like sheets and towels, add a few backups to your registry. Anything that's in heavy rotation will wear out extra fast and need to be replaced more often. You'll be grateful to have a few extra sets when they kick the bucket.

270.

Register for more items than guests. While you don't want to register for things you don't need, aim to register for 50 percent more gifts than guests. (If you're inviting one hundred people, your registry should have about 150 items on it.) Throwing in a few additional products gives your guests more variety to choose from, and when the procrastinators finally get around to purchasing a gift there will still be plenty of options left and they'll be less likely to go off-registry.

271.

Feel your flatware. It makes sense to do your registry research from the comfort of your home (you can pore over reviews without a registry consultant present), but there are some things you should definitely get your hands on first. If you're registering for a high-touch item, like everyday flatware, try to get into a store to pick it up and feel the weight distribution. You don't want to spend the next ten years eating off a fork that doesn't feel right.

CHAPTER 4

Attendants and Attire

272.

You don't need a wedding party. Yes, most weddings have some form of attendants—be that bridesmaids and groomsmen, bridesmen and groomswomen, or a mixed wedding party without any traditional titles—but that doesn't mean *yours* has to. Keep it simple with just your partner or pick one attendant each and call it a day. You can still have bachelor parties and VIP guests with special honors, just forgo the titles and the logistics that come with them.

273.

Relationships trump tradition. None of the "rules" dictating evenly matched gendered wedding parties are written in stone. A male best friend or brother can have the honor of being a bridesman, and the same logic applies to groomswomen (or however your wedding party would like to be identified). No one is going to gawk if you have twelve people on your side of the aisle while your partner only has three. (It's much more awkward to invite nine acquaintances to be in your wedding party solely to even things out.) This goes for outfits too. Don't ask your masculine of center or nonbinary friend to wear a bridesmaid dress just to match everyone else. The pictures aren't worth their discomfort.

274.

Get creative with roles to honor the people you love. Wedding parties tend to be homogenous: friends and relatives who are roughly your age and a few young children. But, if you're close with your grandma, there's nothing that says she can't be your flower girl (it's been done before!), or that your favorite uncle can't be your flower boy with your college roommate as ring bearer. Inviting loved ones to participate in your ceremony in non-traditional ways can allow you to honor people who are special to you while adding joy and levity to the occasion.

275.

Give people space to turn down wedding party roles. Asking your closest friend or relative to serve as maid of honor or best man can be a meaningful way to honor them, but be mindful of the financial responsibilities that can come with the request. If, to you, maid of honor means hosting a wedding shower for thirty guests, can your twenty-two-year-old sister foot that bill? Make your expectations known before asking someone to take on a role that could be financially burdensome, then give them space to turn down the job if they need to.

276.

Scrap utilitarian wedding party roles. If you want to ask your sixty-five-year-old uncle who helped raise you to be your best man but aren't sure how that jives with your expectations around best man responsibilities, honor your feelings instead of tradition. The only real job of your wedding party is to stand up next to you on your wedding day and support your marriage (everything else is made up), so let your uncle be your best man and ask your roommate from college to plan your bachelorette party.

277.

Don't assume you know who wants to make a speech. Wedding toasts are often given by members of the wedding party or important family members who aren't necessarily the best public speakers (stage fright is real), so ask your loved ones if they want to give a toast and don't be afraid to cast a wide net. The most heartfelt speech may come from your college roommate who isn't in the wedding party but remembers when you and your partner first met.

278.

Give your wedding party the gift of saving money. Wedding party gifts are often treated as mandatory but are totally optional (a heartfelt note can go a long way toward showing your appreciation). If you want to honor your party with something monetary, consider paying for a service they need for the wedding (hair and makeup) or a wedding day accessory (ties or jewelry) that can help alleviate the cost of being an attendant. It'll be appreciated much more than a trinket.

279.

Play to people's strengths. Traditional wedding party etiquette dictates that the maid of honor oversees wedding shower and bachelorette party logistics but your BFF might not be your most organized friend. Play to the strengths of your group by asking your bestie to be your honorary attendant, then ask your college roommate to take the lead on the bachelorette party. Just make sure you're clear about everyone's roles in advance to avoid any hurt feelings.

280.

Think beyond the wedding party. There are plenty of ways to honor your loved ones without having a wedding party. Honored guests can officiate, give readings, get ready with you the morning of, and act as ushers. And yes, you can still have a wedding shower or bachelor/bachelorette party without a formal wedding party. Put the word out informally to your nearest and dearest and someone will usually take up the cause. (Or heck, you're an adult. There's nothing that says you can't host your own bachelorette party. Etiquette be damned!)

281.

Keep the bachelor(ette) party local. Bachelor and bachelorette parties used to be simple affairs but in the last decade they've gotten wildly more expensive. If it involves a flight and a hotel, you could be unknowingly asking your friends to spend $1,000 on a mandatory vacation they wouldn't otherwise take. And while Las Vegas might seem like the obvious choice to get out of town, it's not for everyone. Do your friends like gambling? Drinking? Large crowds? If not, something more low-key might be a better fit.

282.

Assign bachelor and bachelorette buddies. Not every bachelor or bachelorette party is going to get out of hand, but it's better to be prepared than not. Make sure everyone has an accountability buddy for the evening or weekend. Pair your most responsible friends with the ones who are more likely to push the envelope so that no one gets lost, goes to jail, or ends up flirting with a Chippendales dancer.

283.

Be realistic about children in your wedding ceremony. Kids in wedding ceremonies are unpredictable (very cute, but unpredictable). Be realistic about your expectations with small children. Kids get excited about the idea of being in a wedding ceremony but can get anxious or nervous when the responsibility settles in. Is your intended flower child or ring bearer normally good in a crowd? Are they okay with lots of attention? Will you be alright if they bail at the last minute? If not, it may be better if they skip the honorary activity.

284.

Hire a wrangler for your pet if they're in the wedding. Dog ring bearers might be the cutest trend to come out of the twenty-first century, second only to flower girl grandmas. If you and your partner have a beloved pet that you want to include in your wedding party, know that animals and big parties don't always mix. If you want to invite Fido, make sure you have a designated caretaker to get him to and from the wedding (and/or to watch him during the reception if you have a venue that allows dogs). The last thing you want to have to do on your wedding day is form a search party for a puppy wearing a flower crown.

285.

Utilize free in-house services to help style your wedding party. The wedding industry really wants to believe that you have strong feelings about how your wedding party looks, but…you might not. And that's okay! You can let someone else do the work by taking advantage of online bridesmaid stores like Brideside.com. They have in-house stylists who can help put together a wedding party look even if you don't know exactly what you want (and they'll make sure everyone orders their stuff in time too, so you don't get stuck sending the reminders).

286.

Use *eShakti* for customizable bridesmaid dresses. For equal to or less than the cost of a traditional bridesmaid dress, you can customize a number of gowns on eShakti.com with different necklines, sleeve lengths, and dress lengths. You simply choose a baseline design and then your wedding party can customize the look to their comfort level, adding sleeves, changing a scoop neck to a V-neck, or shortening the length. *eShakti* goes up to size 36W or 6X so it's also a great choice for plus-size bridesmaids.

287.

Proceed with caution when ordering straight from the factory. You'll find a ton of online results for wedding gowns and bridesmaid dresses sold straight from factories in China, but those dresses can be hit or miss, so do your research before you buy. Third-party reviews should tell you whether or not a company is reputable but, more often than not, you'll be better served by a really great sale at your local bridal store than one of these online shops.

288.

Choose fabrics that are seasonally appropriate. When choosing your and your wedding party's attire, keep your climate in mind. Getting married in the summer? Opt for light fabrics that breathe well (jersey cotton or chiffon for dresses, linen or seersucker for suits). If it's going to be cold, choose heavier fabrics (satin or velvet for dresses, wool for suits), and remember a cover-up for bare arms!

289.

Grab a paint swatch to help communicate colors. Mix-and-match outfits give your wedding party the freedom to wear something they genuinely like while keeping the overall look cohesive, but sometimes that freedom can make things more complicated. (Coral can be both orange *and* pink, so how many clarifying texts do you want to field as your wedding party tries to figure out which one you wanted?) To make things easier, send them a paint swatch from a hardware store as reference colors. The coordinating hues will automatically complement each other, making your wedding party look professionally styled.

290.

Let your bridesmaids rent their dresses. Even if you try really hard to choose a bridesmaid dress that your attendants can wear again, it's unlikely they'll ever have need for a full-length coral chiffon gown. Online rental shops like RenttheRunway.com can be a cost-effective and less wasteful alternative to buying, especially if you're looking at dresses that have limited post-wedding versatility. Dress rentals cost anywhere from $50 to a few hundred dollars and include everything from traditional bridesmaid dresses to high-end couture gowns.

291.

Wait until November to buy bridesmaid dresses. If you're opting for traditional bridesmaid dresses and your timeline allows, wait for Black Friday and Cyber Monday sales. The wedding industry has finally hopped on board these retail holidays and many of the big chain stores offer discounts of 20 percent or more (which in wedding land can save you a lot!). Just remember, if you're trying to save money, it helps to be flexible. Sometimes less popular colors and designs will be more steeply discounted than the hot silhouette of the moment.

292.

Order a sample before committing to an unknown brides-maid dress supplier. Much like wedding dresses, there are lots of straight-from-the-factory bridesmaid dress shops online, but the quality for those suppliers is also hit or miss. Before instructing your wedding party to order dresses from one of these online retailers, get a sample made in a size that fits at least one of your bridesmaids and have her try it on. And make sure you pay careful attention to the return policy in case it doesn't work out.

293.

Rent suits from the same place to get a group discount. It doesn't always make sense to buy suits, especially if the plan involves something less practical for future use, like a unique fabric or a nonstandard suit color. In those cases, rentals are the way to go. As you research your rental options, also look at the fine print of your perks. Some places offer a free rental for the groom(s) if a certain number of groomsmen rent their suits or tuxes there, while others will give the groom(s) their suit(s) to keep.

294.

Online clothing rental isn't always a gamble. Online suit and tux rental companies usually have more modern styles, but it can feel like a gamble to rent a suit sight unseen for something as important as your wedding. Take advantage of free at-home try-ons from places like TheBlackTux.com or GenerationTux.com. You just submit your measurements and the rental company will send you a suit or tux to try out for forty-eight hours. And not every online rental company is exclusively digital! Check their website to see if they have any local showrooms where you can try on a suit in person.

295.

Weight loss is not a mandatory to-do list item. From the moment you get engaged, the wedding industry will inundate you with tips and tricks on how to start "shredding for the wedding." It can start to feel like wedding weight loss is an absolute requirement. But it's not! While it's obviously fine if you *want* to adopt a fitness routine or new health regimen, that doesn't mean you need to transform into a new person just to get married. A "wedding body" belongs to anyone standing up and committing themselves to their partner.

Hack the Search for the Perfect Wedding Dress

Wedding dresses are expensive, and there's a ton of pressure to find "the one." These tips can help you feel more empowered in the search process (and help you find something you really love):

296. Perfect outfits are different for everyone. Think your perfect outfit might not actually be a wedding dress at all? Consider how you dress in your everyday life and figure out the upscaled version of that. Your ideal wedding outfit may end up being a fitted jumpsuit, a crop top with a ball gown skirt, or an agender suit.

297. Not into bridal white? Anything can be a wedding outfit if you're the person getting married. Expand your search to other formal attire like evening gowns, bridesmaid dresses, and non-white wedding dresses.

298. Remember the designer! When you see a picture of a dress you like online or in a magazine, jot down the name of the designer for when you start shopping.

299. Make some phone calls right away. Interested in heading to a specific boutique or salon? Call ahead to make sure their standard sample sizes will work for you.

300. Just shop. Schedule a day to shop without buying (and make sure you tell the sales associate up front!), that way you won't feel pressured to make a decision on the spot.

301. Move on. Is your salesperson a bit pushy? Speaking about your body in a way that makes you feel bad? Not listening? Feel free to (politely) ask for someone else or move on to another salon altogether.

302. Take advantage of online options. Order a handful of dresses from stores like BHLDN.com or Nordstrom.com so you can try them on in the comfort of your own home, then return the ones you don't want.

303. It doesn't hurt to ask. If you see a dress you love online but can't find it in stores or in your size, check with your local bridal salon to see if the designer will send samples so you can try them on in person.

304. It's new to you! For a significant discount, shop sample gowns and gently used wedding dresses on sites like PreOwnedWeddingDresses .com or BorrowingMagnolia.com.

305. Don't order a dress that's too small with the idea that you'll lose weight. It's often easier (and less stressful!) to have a dress altered to be made smaller than it is to have it made more than a few inches larger.

306.

Shop _Etsy_ for affordable custom wedding gowns. _Etsy_ might be best known for crafty home décor, but it can also be a treasure trove of affordable wedding accoutrements (printable invitation templates, cake toppers, tabletop decorations, and so on). You can also find a bevy of independent fashion designers selling made-to-measure custom wedding gowns for only a few hundred dollars. Just be sure to check the reviews and make sure there are customer photos that showcase the product so you can get a sense of the real thing.

307.

Shop trunk shows to find discounted dresses from your favorite designer. Unless you live in a big city with lots of wedding dress salons, your local bridal shop probably only carries a handful of designs from each wedding dress designer. If you want the opportunity to shop a broader collection, look for trunk shows (when dress designers take their show on the road and bring their collection to your city) that might be coming to town. Most trunk shows happen in the first half of the year and include steep discounts on gowns if you're able to buy on the spot.

308.

Seek out plus-size dress stores. Shopping for a wedding dress can be challenging for anyone who doesn't fit into sample sizes. How are you supposed to know what looks good if you can't try the dresses on? While national chains like David's Bridal usually carry plus-size sample dresses in-store, you may be better served by a shop that caters specifically to plus-size brides. Check Google to see if there's one in your area, like Olivia's Bridal House in Houston, Strut Bridal Salon in Southern California, or Ivory & Main in New York.

309.

Shop online for more size inclusivity. Most wedding dress salons carry only a small selection of sample size gowns in-house but many (if not most) popular wedding dress designers offer styles up to a size 32W or higher. So if you're striking out in-person, head online. If you're on a strict budget, *Torrid* and *ASOS Curve* both carry bridal collections, and *eShakti* will let you build a gown custom to your measurements. The logistics of shopping for a dress you can't try on in-person are more challenging, but you'll be able to shop from a broader selection of styles.

310.

Choose an easy-to-search brand if you want to resell your wedding dress. If you're hoping to recoup some of the cost of your wedding dress, you may be able to resell it online (though it's best not to count on it). Sites like Stillwhite.com, BorrowingMagnolia.com, NearlyNewlywed.com, and PreOwnedWeddingDresses.com all make it easy to find pre-owned wedding dresses at a discount, but your chances of successfully reselling are greater if you buy a dress with a familiar brand name that customers might be searching for rather than a custom dress or an indie gown.

311.

Design a completely custom wedding dress online. If you can't find the right wedding dress in stores, you can design a custom dress online at DressAnomalie.com for around $1,200 to $1,600. Start with the style quiz, then work with a stylist to customize a dress to your specifications. Since custom dresses are made-to-measure, they are more size inclusive and you'll also have a better chance of not needing alterations.

312.

Don't buy an ill-fitting sample dress. Sample sales can be a great way to save on a designer you love but can't afford. However, steer clear of the way-too-big dress that needs to be taken in several inches to fit. To make a large dress smaller, the person doing the alterations will need to take it apart and put it back together, which can get expensive fast. A general guideline: One size too big (two at the very most) is about as oversized as you'll want to get.

313.

A *little* small is okay when dress shopping. If you find a dress or outfit you love and it's just a little snug, there's usually an inch or two of wiggle room built into the seams of garments. Seamstresses can easily let them out without having to reconstruct the entire garment. Anything more than that and things start to get complicated and expensive. If you can get it to zip, you should be fine.

314.

Add a corset back for more affordable tailoring on your wedding dress. Traditional wedding dress shopping timelines suggest buying your dress six months to a year before your wedding, which means your body may change before your actual wedding day. If you need to have your dress taken out a bit but don't want to spring for a full reconstruction, ask your seamstress to put in a corset back. They're more affordable and make it easier to make small adjustments to your dress size the day of.

315.

Wear an off-the-rack silver or gold evening gown. Wedding dresses often cost anywhere between $1,500 to $5,000 and up. If you're not attached to the idea of a white bridal gown but don't want to break with tradition completely, search for a silver or gold evening gown that you can buy off the rack. Sites like Nordstrom.com, SaksOff5th.com, and LastCall.com have a variety of glitzy and glamorous evening gowns that are wedding appropriate and only cost a few hundred dollars.

316.

Quality tailoring can make an affordable outfit look expensive. If you buy off the rack (whether it's a suit, dress, or any other outfit combination), set aside some funds for expert tailoring. Call a local wedding dress shop or suit store and ask if they have anyone they recommend (even if you didn't buy your outfit there). Bonus: If you find a tailor you love, you can continue using them well beyond the wedding.

317.

Shop around before committing to alterations. If you buy a suit from a place that specializes in formal attire or a dress from a dedicated wedding salon, they may have an in-house person who handles tailoring. While it can make things easier to keep alterations in-house, it can also be more expensive (especially if you only need light alterations and the salon has a minimum charge). Ask if they'll allow you to shop around and then see if a local tailor can do the work you need.

318.

Have a backup for your bustle. Wedding dresses often have a train in the back for dramatic effect while walking down the aisle. Because trains aren't always conducive to dancing, designers and tailors usually include an option to bustle (that's where you pin up the train to the back of your dress so you don't trip on it while dancing). But delicate bustles can break (and sometimes are too complicated for slightly tipsy people to remember how to do), so reinforce your train with a hidden safety pin as backup to avoid having to hold up your dress all night.

319.

Avoid new shoe pitfalls by roughing up the soles. New shoes on a rented dance floor can make for a slippery disaster. If you've opted for a fresh pair of wedding kicks, take a piece of sandpaper to the bottoms first. Sanding the soles will make the surface less slick and prevent you from taking any unnecessary falls. Don't forget to practice walking in them too (a lot). The day to break in fancy footwear is not your wedding day. And, for that matter, if you never wear heels, don't start now. Fancy flats exist for a reason.

320.

Use veil weights. Wind can make for dramatic veil photos, but you don't want your accessories obscuring your face when you're trying to commit yourself to your partner for the rest of your lives. If there's a chance of wind, purchase veil weights to keep your veil from blowing around. The removable magnets cost about $20 (or you can DIY with hot glue, strong magnets, and a decorative element to cover them up).

321.

Keep new skincare routines to a minimum. Your wedding can be a great excuse to settle into a self-care routine, but not all treatments will leave you with an immediate glow (post-facial redness and breakouts are not unheard of). If you opt to explore new skincare routines, makeup, or spa treatments, give your skin plenty of time to adjust and adapt. Adverse reactions can take a few weeks to calm down, so be mindful (and always ask a pro first) before you schedule something you've never tried before.

322.

Wear comfy shoes with a ball gown. Wedding shoes are often synonymous with fancy, ornate high heels, but if you're wearing a long dress that obscures your feet (particularly a ball gown) no one will ever see what you're wearing. Skip the pain and opt for comfortable shoes that you can wear all night, or wear the fancy shoes for photos then switch to flats for dancing.

323.

Know the difference between a suit and a tuxedo. If you hear the word "tuxedo" and immediately think of James Bond's white coat, you're not alone. However, the difference between a suit and a tuxedo is rather subtle to the untrained eye. Tuxedos have satin detailing, usually along the lapels, buttons, and a stripe down the pant legs. Suits, on the other hand, don't have any satin and the buttons are usually plastic or covered with a fabric that matches the rest of the jacket. Tuxedo pants also don't have belt loops, so if you normally wear a belt, get ready to don suspenders.

324.

Never button the bottom button on a suit jacket. There's an easy way to remember which buttons to close on a three-button suit: "Sometimes, Always, Never." If you're wearing a three-button suit jacket, you can button the top button at your discretion (based on how the suit looks), then always button the middle but never the bottom button. For two-button jackets, the rule is similar: When closing the jacket, button the top and skip the bottom.

325.

Invest in quality undergarments if you're wearing a strapless dress. Wedding dresses cost as much as they do in part because of the internal structure necessary to hold up all that fabric. This means in some cases you may be able to get away with less than your normal amount of support wear. But if you're well-endowed (and especially if you're wearing a strapless dress), invest in a quality undergarment, like a supportive longline bra. Good undergarments can help affordable dresses fit like more expensive gowns (and they can help save on alterations too).

326.

Don't pay for a veil you could easily DIY. Unless you have visions of a detailed veil with lots of beading or delicate lace edges, chances are you'll be spending lots of money on what amounts to a piece of fabric attached to a comb. While not every DIY project is worth the effort, simple wedding veils are surprisingly easy to make and a handmade version can cost less than $20. Even the more complex designs are still achievable with some time, patience, and video tutorials.

Ten Alternative Bachelor and Bachelorette Party Ideas

Bachelor and bachelorette parties have gotten way more complicated and expensive than they need to be. If strip clubs, penis straws, and Vegas aren't your thing, consider one of these ideas instead:

327. **Have an *Airbnb* sleepover.** With enough people, a luxury *Airbnb* can end up costing less than a hotel. So queue up your favorite movie, put together a playlist, grab some wine, and bond with your wedding party like it's a middle school sleepover.

328. **Go on a brewery tour.** See if your town has a brewery that offers tastings. Sign up for a private group event or hop around to different breweries for an ad-hoc beer tour.

329. **Charter a sailboat.** If you live somewhere near the water, you can charter a sailboat for an afternoon for a few hundred dollars. Bring a picnic and host a dockside wine and cheese pairing. But remember the Dramamine (just in case!).

330. **Host an at-home cooking party.** Instead of going out for dinner, eat in with a private cooking party. You can host at your party location (home, vacation rental) or, if you don't want to bother with cleanup, look for cooking schools with private classes on-site.

331. **Get crafty and make something.** You can host your own crafting party (bring your own BeDazzler, anyone?) or hire a professional to teach a fun activity like jacket painting or macramé home décor.

332. **Go glamping.** Are your friends the outdoorsy type? Find a campground that offers upscale tents and go glamping for the weekend. S'mores, campfire tales, and nature walks are the name of the game.

333. Get mystical. Hire an astrologer, medium, or tarot card reader and get the group's fortunes read. You can follow up your witchy activities with a viewing of *Practical Magic* and some Ouija board action.

334. **Have a spa day.** Check yourselves into a local spa for a day of pampering, or do it at home. You can hire on-call aestheticians for spa treatments or get a manicurist to give your group a funky nail art treatment.

335. **Take a dance class.** Nothing gets endorphins going quite like a dance class. You can stick with a classic genre like hip-hop, learn choreography to your favorite song, or get sensual with a pole dancing class.

336. **Do anything that was fun when you were twelve years old.** Paintball. Capture the flag. Making friendship bracelets. When you're in a group that spans decades of friendship, nostalgia can be an instant bonding mechanism.

337.

Make your bustle do double duty. If you're working with a professional to have a bustle put onto a dress, ask if your seamstress can sew in two different lengths: one for heels and one for bare feet. That way, when you take off your shoes in the middle of the dance floor, your dress won't drag on the ground.

338.

Hide the pin when attaching a boutonniere. When given a straight pin and a boutonniere, most people do what you'd think they'd do—insert the pin horizontally (that is, with the pin parallel to the floor). But that almost guarantees you'll have a pin showing in all your photos. Instead, insert the straight pin vertically, starting from the back of your lapel and working it through the body of the boutonniere. The vertical pin covers more of the boutonniere's length, making it more secure while keeping it hidden inside your jacket.

339.

Use an earring back to avoid injury. People often pin corsages and boutonnieres on the outside of their jacket or top with the end of the pin facing out to keep from being poked. You can avoid any potential pin mishaps by purchasing a small container of rubber earring backs and sticking them on the ends of your straight pins after the arrangement has been attached to your garment. Then the pin will be hidden on the inside of your garment *and* you won't get poked.

340.

Give your beard time to relax. If you have a beard, schedule a trim for about a week before your wedding day (or three to four days out if your beard is on the shorter side). This gives your facial hair some time to relax. And avoid any drastic changes too close to the day of. Any experimenting should happen with plenty of time to change your mind. The goal is to show up looking like the most polished version of yourself, not like an entirely different person.

341.

Shop queer-owned stores for a bespoke suit. If you're nonbinary or masculine of center and want to wear a suit for your wedding, you don't have to settle for an ill-fitting men's suit or a too-fitted women's suit. Queer-owned stores like BindleandKeep.com and DuchessClothier.com were created to fill that gap and you can get a custom two-piece suit starting at just under $900.

342.

Hack an off-the-rack suit for nonbinary style. If you identify as nonbinary or masculine of center and plan on wearing a suit or tux but can't afford the price of a custom suit, you can buy a men's suit off the rack and take it to a queer-friendly tailor for alterations. If you want to shop in person, Men's Wearhouse and Indochino have a wide selection of styles. (Try calling ahead and asking to work with a sales associate who has experience with LGBTQ customers.) Online, you can find modern and androgynous styles at ASOS.com and Wildfang.com.

343.

Wear a suit you already own. If you don't have a nice suit in your closet, a wedding is the perfect excuse to invest in a quality piece you'll wear again. But there's no need to go out and purchase a brand-new suit just for the sake of it. You can spruce up an existing suit with a new shirt, tie, pocket square, and pair of socks. And with the money you'll save on the suit, you can spring for heirloom accessories.

344.

Scratch boutonnieres from your floral quote. If you're working with a florist, or even doing your own flowers, boutonnieres and corsages are usually in the standard wedding flower package. But you don't need them. For suit adornment, ask your wedding party to don pocket squares. Most of the time boutonnieres won't be missed and you can easily cut $75 or more off your flower bill.

345.

Let an app find hair and makeup artists for you. Service-based wedding vendors like makeup artists and hair stylists often book their business through word of mouth, but if you don't know anyone who's recently gotten married, how do you find someone? Sites like Glamsquad.com and StyleBee.com are kind of like the Uber of hair and makeup. Just enter your event needs, select from available artists, and book instantly.

346.

Wear 20 percent more makeup. How you choose to wear your makeup (if any at all) is up to you—you want to make sure you feel like yourself—but if photography is a priority, aim to apply 20 percent more than you'd normally wear. If you're considering light foundation, throw on an additional layer. If you were going to wear a light lipstick, consider upping the opacity. Photos tend to downplay makeup, so a little extra will make you look like your normal self in pictures.

347.

Keep your hair dirty for updos. If your hair is straight or wavy, it will style better with a little dirt and oil in it, so if you're getting your hair professionally done, it's recommended that you wash your hair the day before. If you have textured hair in its natural state, you may even want to schedule your appointment for the day before (for braided styles or twist outs). Not sure where your hair falls? Ask your hairdresser for their recommended styling tips and timeline.

348.

Check your makeup artist's kit. Professional makeup artists should have the supplies to work with a variety of skin types and tones. But not all do! Before hiring anyone, check the artist's portfolio to see if they've worked on people with your skin tone or if they can speak to dry and oily skin, and then confirm that their kit is fully stocked. Professional artists should be able to answer "yes" confidently.

349.

Time your hair and makeup trial for scheduling accuracy. If you've never gotten your hair or makeup done professionally, it can be difficult to assess how much time you'll need to set aside for primping on your wedding day. While your hair or makeup artist should be able to give you a rough time estimate, set a timer during your trial to get a more accurate number, then factor that into your preparation timeline.

350.

Don't go for mainstream nude. Nude lipstick that's the same color as your skin will wash you out. Instead, opt for a color that's closer to your natural lip color, like rose, mauve, berry, or brown (depending on your skin tone). If you aren't finding your shade? Black-owned cosmetic companies like Mented, Pat McGrath, and Fenty Beauty sell lipsticks specifically formulated for darker skin tones. And remember, most drugstores and cosmetic shops offer returns on makeup products (yup, even if you opened it) within thirty or sixty days, so remember to keep those receipts, then play around until you find a shade that works.

351.

Hit up your local Drybar. If you've got straight or wavy hair and the idea of a traditional wedding updo makes you cringe, see if there are any Drybar salons in your area. Drybar specializes in blowouts (shampoo plus styled blow-dry) for around $50 and low-key updos for $100, so you can still get your hair done professionally the morning of your wedding. That said, if you have textured hair, you may want to skip the Drybar and opt for a salon that has experience with textured hairstyles. Check *Instagram* for salons with tags that speak to multicultural, Black, textured, curly, or natural hair.

352.

Rent designer accessories for way less. If you have champagne jewelry taste but don't want to spend big bucks on something you'll never wear again, you can rent designer pieces from brands like Oscar de la Renta and Kate Spade on RenttheRunway.com. (They even have dedicated wedding accessories like veils and hair combs.) Skip the wedding section and filter your search results by color and formality to see a broader range of styles.

353.

Get a lab-grown diamond. If you're shopping for a wedding band (or buying a post-engagement ring), look for lab-grown diamonds and gemstones. They are chemically and physically the exact same as earth-mined diamonds with a much lower price tag and none of the ethical conflicts. You can only tell the difference under a microscope, and even then a trained specialist would struggle to find a difference in quality.

354.

Don't go for the gold (wedding ring, that is). Platinum, silver, and gold aren't the only materials for wedding rings. You can find affordable wedding bands made of titanium, tungsten carbide, and even silicone. These range in price from $20 for a silicone band to $250 and up for tungsten carbide on sites like ManlyBands.com. But beware the $20 tungsten rings you find on *Amazon*. The material used to bind the tungsten in those rings isn't jewelry grade, which means they are more likely to tarnish and may even cause an allergic reaction.

355.

Get a travel ring for your honeymoon. If you're planning on traveling after you get married, consider opting for an inexpensive ring that you can take with you. You won't want to be responsible for expensive jewelry that you're not used to wearing while you're out and about in unfamiliar territory. (Plus, metal rings can get damaged in pools and oceans.) You can buy a fake diamond ring online for under $25, or forgo the sparkles altogether and get a silicone wedding band from EnsoRings.com or Qalo.com for the same price.

356.

Look for the free return. The wedding industry is old-fashioned, which means that online businesses have to work extra hard to gain your loyalty. For that reason, many online shops (especially for big-ticket items like jewelry) offer generous return policies. When you're comparing options, make sure to check the return policies. The risk-free option might be a safer bet than the more affordable alternative.

357.

Consider jewelry insurance. If you have an engagement ring, it may be covered under your homeowners or renters insurance policy—but only up to a certain amount. Jewelry is considered high value and easy to lose, so many policies cap the coverage amount at $1,000 or $2,000. If yours is worth more than that, consider adding extra coverage to your policy or taking out a separate jewelry insurance policy. Policies cost anywhere from $50 to $100 a year (give or take depending on the value of your ring).

358.

Ask your jeweler if they offer free appraisals. The value of your ring may actually be more than you paid for it, which could increase your insurance premium but also your payout if it gets lost. However, you'll only know if you get it professionally appraised. Before spending $100 to have your jewelry inspected, ask the store where you bought it if they have any free perks. Some stores offer loyalty services like free appraisals and cleanings on any rings they've sold.

359.

Easily make at-home jewelry cleaner with products you already have. Rings can get dingy quickly (particularly if they have a lot of small details), but you don't need one of those fancy ring cleaners they sell at the jewelers. Just mix a small amount of dish soap with warm water and soak your ring, then use a soft toothbrush to gently scrub the stone and setting. Voilà! Instant sparkle!

CHAPTER 5

Reception and Décor

360.

Call on your community for rentals. Before you sink a large chunk of change into rented tables and chairs, look to your local community. If you're a member of a church or have connections to your local high school, you may be able to borrow chairs and tables from them. They probably won't be as high end as what you'd get from a rental company, but free is free (and that's what tablecloths are for).

361.

You can rent almost anything. If you're working with a raw space and need to bring in your own furniture (or have your heart set on a specific piece of décor) but don't want to end up with a velvet settee in your home after the wedding, remember that almost anything can be rented. This includes any kind of furniture you can imagine as well as statement décor. And shop around! More modern and non-traditional rental companies will have updated furniture that doesn't give you a bad prom flashback.

362.

Have your chairs perform double duty. If your ceremony and reception are in the same area, don't rent twice as many chairs as you need. Instead, set out chairs for the ceremony, then ask a handful of pre-appointed volunteers to bring them back into the reception space when the ceremony is over. Just make sure the trip is a short one so that your guests aren't being asked to do too much heavy lifting in their formal attire.

363.

Get a rain plan tent. If you're planning an outdoor wedding and there's even a small chance of rain, you'll want a backup plan (for your sanity alone). A rain plan tent requires a deposit to hold it but you only have to pay the balance if you actually end up using it. You'll spend more money than you would without a tent, but it's a fair price to pay for peace of mind.

364.

Use a sweetheart table to get out of choosing who sits at the VIP table. If you have tricky family dynamics to negotiate (divorced parents, for example) and you don't want to choose a side at the reception, opt for a sweetheart table for just you and your partner. It'll give you a chance to decompress during dinner and you won't have to play favorites.

365.

Seat divorced parents at their own tables. Divorced parents aren't necessarily always at odds with each other—if they get along well, by all means seat them at the same table—but if there's tension between your parents, you can avoid conflict by allowing each of them to host their own tables. Then put a buffer between those tables. With a bit of space, you limit the frequency with which they have to interact.

366.

Add a memorial table to honor deceased loved ones. Weddings can be bittersweet if you've lost close friends or family. Honor them in whatever way feels most authentic to you. A locket on your bouquet with a photo inside, a memorial table with photos and tokens of remembrance, an empty seat at a reception table with flowers in your loved one's place, or a special moment of silence during the ceremony are just a few of the ways you can pay tribute to those who are no longer with us.

367.

Don't keep your guests waiting for food. There are plenty of wedding rules you can break. The one you should never mess with? Don't keep your guests hungry. Even if you're serving non-traditional catering (potluck, for example), remember to have light bites on hand for any gaps between the ceremony and dinner (a cheese tray or charcuterie is great for this).

368.

Choose a food truck that can serve a crowd. Food trucks can be a great solution when you're working with a venue that doesn't have a built-in kitchen (and you can get more culinary options than a standard wedding menu might offer), but do your due diligence and make sure whoever you're working with is experienced in serving large crowds. And opt for a menu that can be cooked in batches so your guests don't have to wait in a huge line for their meal to be prepared.

369.

Stagger your serving time. If you're serving buffet style, assign someone to call people up by table so you don't end up with a huge line behind the food (and if you can, line people up on both sides of the table to double your line speed). You and your partner should eat first, then the wedding party and any VIP guests. This gives anyone who needs to make a toast the option to finish their dinner before they get up and speak. (Bonus: A little food in the belly can sober up a tipsy groomsman or parent before toast time.)

370.

Feed your vendors a hot meal. Vendors often work long, arduous days, especially on-the-ground folks like wedding photographers and day-of coordinators. Remember to feed them! Include any day-of vendors in your catering estimate and try to feed them the same food you're serving your guests (some venues might have a "vendor meal" option, but a hot dinner is more re-energizing after a long day and will lead to better work).

371.

Use an alcohol calculator. If you're DIYing your wedding alcohol, the last thing you want is to make a mid-celebration trip to the store to secure more provisions. Evite.com has an interactive alcohol calculator that lets you plug in the length of your wedding and the number of guests you're expecting (including whether they're light, average, or heavy drinkers) and then instantly computes what you'll need to buy. APracticalWedding.com also has an in-depth resource on which mixers to purchase, how many bartenders to hire, and how to modify your alcohol calculations based on the particulars of your wedding.

372.

Rent plenty of glasses. People seldom use just one drinking glass for the night (cups get put down, drinks get abandoned), so if you're providing your own drinkware or calculating your own rental needs, aim for five to six drinking glasses per person. If you can't afford the extra drinkware, provide your guests with a way to mark their glasses so they can keep track of them throughout the night.

373.

Get compostable plates if you aren't renting. If you're getting married in a location where rentals wouldn't make sense (a campground wedding, for example) but want something a little fancier than paper plates, you can buy beautiful compostable bamboo or palm leaf servingware for sixty cents to $1 per plate. SmartyHadAParty.com has a wide selection of disposable and compostable dinnerware, with wedding packages (plates, knives, forks, and spoons) starting at around $150 for one hundred guests.

374.

Pass out drinks at the beginning. Guests have a habit of rushing the bar right after the ceremony, but long lines can be a buzzkill. While you don't need bartenders roaming the floor all night, it can be helpful to have someone passing out cocktails or taking drink orders during cocktail hour to avoid a crowded bar. Batch cocktails served in dispensers or tubs filled with beer and wine (as allowed by your venue and local laws) can also alleviate the barback burden.

375.

Ditch the champagne toast. The champagne toast is a stalwart wedding tradition, but when you factor in the cost of bottles, pouring service, and renting additional glassware, you could be looking at a cost of $2 to $7 per person (depending on how nice the champagne is). Save a few hundred dollars and have your guests toast you with whatever drink they have in hand.

376.

Get creative with your bar setup. You can save a lot of money by skipping the full open bar and serving beer, wine, and a signature cocktail, or by having a limited open bar (i.e., the first two hours are free and then it's cash). If your venue allows, you can always ask your caterer if you can BYOB and either hire or provide your own bartender. And if the budget is particularly restricted, a cash bar won't *actually* kill anyone.

377.

Avoid lines at the bar with batch cocktails. If you're supplying your own alcohol for your wedding, don't leave it up to your guests to mix their own cocktails. (That's a quick recipe for long lines and drunk guests.) Instead, offer up a few crowd-pleasing pre-mixed cocktails in large dispensers so all your guests have to do is pour. If you're concerned about varying levels of tolerance, you can always batch your mixers and then let guests choose how much alcohol they want to add.

378.

Save your playlist to the cloud. Self-DJing can save you anywhere from $300 to $700 on your reception costs. Just make sure to save your playlist to the cloud in addition to your device so there's a backup in case of technical difficulties or spotty Wi-Fi. (Needing playlist inspiration? There are also tons available online. APracticalWedding.com has playlists for almost every minute of your party.)

379.

Play the classics first to pack the dance floor. When organizing your playlist, start with classics before moving into more contemporary jams. (Anything Motown should do the trick.) Old-school hits appeal to the majority and will pack your dance floor the fastest. Plus, your elderly guests likely won't stick around quite as late as your high school BFFs, so you want to play the crowd-pleasers early.

380.

Skip the tiny details no one will notice. Wedding publications love to focus on small wedding details like table décor, but think about any party you've been to. Do you remember what was on your plate before you sat down? Probably not. Focus on big, impactful backdrops over minutiae. Statement décor will end up in your candid photos and give you the most bang for your buck.

381.

Stand in front of your statement details. If you want it to look like you splurged on an expensive designer, create two statement back-drops, one for your ceremony and one for your reception, then put them where you and your partner will be standing or sitting the longest (behind a sweetheart table, for example). Most of your wedding photos will be laser focused on you and your partner, so you'll get the most mile-age out of décor that's close by.

382.

Seating charts aren't old-fashioned. It's not exactly fun to create a seating chart, so it's understandable if you were hoping to avoid one, but seating charts exist for a reason. While open seating might make sense in some cases, it often leads to awkward encounters among guests (not enough room at tables, significant others needing to split up, and so on). If your reception involves the standard round or long table, consider creating a seating chart for the benefit of your guests. No one wants to have a high school cafeteria flashback at a party.

383.

Visualize your seating chart. Putting together a seating chart usually means arranging and rearranging names until it's just right. It's easier to do that if you can visualize the room. Software like WeddingWire.com's seating chart tool lets you create a custom room layout with different table types and assign guests accordingly. You can also do it the low-tech way with a piece of paper and Post-it Notes.

Ten of the Most Affordable DIY Materials

Once you calculate the cost to make one hundred of anything, DIY projects aren't always money savers, but these creative materials give a ton of bang for your buck and are easily purchased in bulk:

384. Balloons. Balloon garlands have come a long way since your high school graduation. When assembled in large quantities with varying colors and sizes, they can make a huge statement.

385. Paper. The most affordable and versatile craft material is paper. Make large paper flowers, oversized origami, or create cool garlands out of small pieces of folded paper. Just remember to give yourself lots of time for execution!

386. Lumber. Have a saw handy? Make a few angled cuts in standard lumber and you can create cool geometric backdrops with very little material. Think oversized hexagons or triangles assembled into an abstract shape.

387. Honeycomb décor. You can find honeycomb décor in the aisles of almost any party supply store. If you don't love the out-of-the-box look, add spray paint or use adhesive to add glitter or confetti. Hang them from the ceiling, use them as centerpieces, or string a bunch together for an abstract garland.

388. Paint. Make enough of anything the same color and you've got yourself a cohesive décor statement. Use painter's tape to create clean lines and geometric designs to make thrifted, recycled, or dollar store décor look like their more expensive counterparts.

389. **Succulents.** Hardy plants like succulents are often available in miniature sizes for a dollar or two each. When put together, they can make an impactful centerpiece, escort card station, or place setting. Plus, they're sustainable, and your guests can take them home after the wedding!

390. **Thrifted china.** If you have a long engagement and can commit the time (and storage) to treasure hunting, thrifted china makes for an eclectic and fun table setting.

391. **Tea lights and taper candles.** Skip the bulkier pillar candles (which can be expensive) and use tea lights or taper candles as centerpieces. Candle holders can be bought or rented affordably in bulk, but check your venue's open flame rules before you buy. (You can always use battery-operated candles instead.)

392. **Macramé.** If you can tie a knot, you can create large scale backdrops using nothing but macramé cord and your free time. Or buy pre-made macramé backdrops online and then dye to your desired color.

393. **Fabric.** Craft stores are almost always doling out coupons for 40 percent off a single item, and that includes cuts of fabric. Use bright patterns to create statement backdrops or spruce up your table settings.

394.

Make a flexible seating chart. Seating charts can be beautiful décor *and* they tell your guests where to go, but in the event of last-minute guest list changes, opt for something you can reposition (as opposed to a chart that would need to be re-created from scratch if someone drops out or needs to be moved to a different table). Escort cards are a great way to accomplish this.

395.

Rent more chairs than you need for open seating. If you're not assigning seating at your wedding, rent a few more chairs than you actu- ally need. Without a seating chart, guests aren't guaranteed to split off into perfectly even groups of eight. Renting a few extra chairs helps you avoid awkward seating situations (like having to split up a couple).

396.

Use globe lights to make your photos sparkle. Create a high-impact visual element in all your reception photos with globe lights from the garden section of your local big-box store. The soft glow creates gorgeous photo effects and helps provide ambient light for harder-to-photograph spaces (like dark barns and backyards). Plus, when the wedding is over, you can re-string them in your home or yard. Pro tip: You can rent globe lights from party suppliers for $40 to $50 per string if you'd rather not be saddled with a bunch of globe lights you can't use. (Rented lights are three to four times longer than what you would buy in a store, which means fewer extension cords.)

397.

Capture the memory of your wedding guests with a video booth. Big weddings can mean limited one-on-one time to spend with each of your guests (and the day can go by in such a blur that sometimes it's hard to remember talking to them anyway). SpeechBooth.com gives your loved ones the opportunity to give live video toasts in a photo booth–style setup (i.e., no videographer walking around asking people for toasts). It includes a microphone, tripod, stand, and professional video editing for $599.

398.

Search _Craigslist_ and _Facebook Marketplace_ for used wedding décor. Most people end up with unwanted décor after their wedding (the pitfall of buying or DIYing instead of renting), which means they're willing to sell it for way less than what they paid. Search online resale sites for previously used wedding décor like table numbers, faux florals, centerpiece elements, vases, glassware, and backdrops.

399.

Store silk flowers to avoid dust. High-quality silk flowers and greenery can be almost indistinguishable from the real thing from a few feet away (and are a great alternative to fresh flowers if you want out-of-season blooms or are getting married in a climate that's not fresh flower–friendly). Silk flowers are also dust magnets. Store them in airtight containers to avoid having to clean them extensively before the wedding. You can also use a silk flower spray to refresh any blooms that have lost their luster.

400.

Buy silk flowers at the end of the season. Silk flowers last longer than fresh flowers, but the tradeoff is they can be more expensive (especially if you're buying individual stems from your local craft store). Places like Michaels and JOANN Fabrics and Crafts have frequent sales with deep discounts. You can save 40 to 50 percent if you wait until the end of the season to buy, before they change their inventory. And sign up for promotional texts or emails to be notified of additional discounts (especially the elusive 20 or 40 percent off your whole order).

401.

Forget the party favors. Party favors are expensive. While they were once a stalwart of the modern wedding, not many people want a customized drinking goblet with *your* name and wedding date on it. The easiest way to save money is to skip them altogether. For the people who expect a parting gift, you can always let a handful of guests take home your centerpieces. (Bonus: It means you won't have to store them later.)

402.

Give out consumable or practical party favors. If you have your heart set on giving your guests parting gifts but want to avoid waste, opt for something consumable like baked goods, mini bottles of champagne, flavored salts, infused olive oil, local coffee, or small jars of jam. Alternatively, go super practical and give out small plants (succulents are a hardy favorite), parasols or sunglasses if the wedding is outside, a personalized bottle opener or box of matches, cute measuring spoons, or anything else your guests might use in everyday life.

403.

Don't DIY to save money. Wedding sticker shock is real, and when you compare the costs of goods online to the raw materials, it can seem like DIY is the obvious way to save money. However, once you factor in the cost of trial and error plus the amount of time you'll need to spend on the effort, DIY projects are seldom money savers (and they can eat up a lot of your energy budget). Instead, save the crafting for projects you care about the most. You'll be much less resentful of the time it takes to execute and more likely to see things through to the end.

404.

Repurpose your ceremony flowers. If your ceremony and reception are in separate locations, let your flowers do double duty. Ceremony arrangements can be repurposed as statement pieces in your entryway, at the gift or guest book table, or any other location that could use a little sprucing up. Just make sure you have a plan for transporting them from one location to the next!

405.

Don't block your guests' view. Tall centerpieces are meant to offset high ceilings so the room doesn't feel awkwardly empty, but they can also make it impossible for guests to interact. If you want to fill the vertical space of your venue, float balloons above your tables or hang lights or fabric from the ceiling. If you *do* opt for a tall centerpiece, keep the base narrow so your guests can still see each other.

406.

Carnations are more than just filler. Carnations have gotten a bad reputation in the world of wedding flowers, but when grouped together they can create high-impact décor that mimics more expensive floral varieties like peonies. To avoid a dated 1990s look, skip the round carnation ball and vary the height of your stems (look to more wild and unstructured arrangements for inspiration) and use gold-toned vases instead of glass. You can also string carnation heads from fishing wire for a fun floral backdrop.

407.

Rent what you don't want to keep. When considering the cost of rentals versus buying your wedding décor, remember that anything you buy will need to be stored somewhere after the wedding. (There's no guarantee you'll be able to resell your wedding goods, so don't bank on that as your plan.) If you don't want it in your house or garage after the wedding, don't buy it.

408.

Ask for black linens. If linens are included with your venue, ask if you can get black tablecloths instead of white ones. White is more easily stained and can be see-through, while black linens lend a sophisticated and rich vibe to your tables. Since black is considered a standard color, it's usually included as a free option, saving money over the cost of more colorful linens.

409.

Spring for colorful napkins. Your guests are more likely to notice and remember the color of your napkins than almost anything else you put out on your tables thanks to their prominent placement and frequent use throughout the night, so if you're looking to include a pop of color in your décor, do it there. Plus, colorful napkins often cost the same (maybe a few cents more) as white ones. And you can always get creative! Rent a variety of shades in the same color family for a bohemian tablescape or throw a pattern or texture into the mix to spruce up your table décor.

410.

Yes, it's cheaper to buy linens (but not always better). If you do the math, it's significantly cheaper to buy table linens than it is to rent them (on average it costs $10 to $12 to rent a basic tablecloth and $6 to $8 to buy the equivalent), but rental companies include storage, laundering, and delivery in their prices (freshly unboxed tablecloths are usually filled with wrinkles that need to be steamed out), so don't forget to take sweat equity into account when running your calculations. Is it worth the savings to store, steam, and launder twenty tablecloths? Only you can answer that! (But seriously, that's a lot of tablecloths to steam.)

411.

Give yourself a hard deadline for any DIY projects, then stick with it. You don't want to be hot gluing your centerpieces two days before your wedding. Ideally, the last two months of wedding planning should be dedicated to tying up loose ends and closing logistical loops. At the very least, try to avoid any crafting in the last few weeks leading up to the wedding (unless it's a project that serves a separate function, like distracting you from pre-wedding anxiety; in which case, craft on!).

412.

Budget double the time for DIY projects. When you find a DIY project online, remember that it was most likely created by a professional crafter who does these kinds of projects all the time, then factor the learning curve into your time estimates. At a minimum, expect any DIY project to take twice as long as you think it might (and maybe even longer than that).

413.

You can pay for DIY knowledge. If you see a décor item you love but there aren't clear instructions for how to make it, reach out to the maker to see if you can pay for a copy of their instructions. A small fee is way better than a lot of time and energy wasted on guesswork (and you'll probably offset the cost by not having to buy materials twice if you mess up the first time).

414.

Have a backup plan for abandoned DIY projects. DIY projects always start out with the best of intentions, but as you move through wedding planning you may discover you don't have the time or energy to execute as many as you'd originally thought. Come up with a backup plan *before* you start any DIY endeavors. Decide if you can live without the project or figure out a purchasable option in advance to avoid a last-minute panic if you choose to switch gears.

415.

Multipurpose is the name of the game. To reduce the number of details you need to buy or make, figure out which décor pieces can perform double duty. Can your place card also be a favor? Can your escort cards be fashioned into a cool entryway display? Can your programs also function as hand fans on a hot day? If you can take a functional piece and display it stylishly, you've just given yourself an extra piece of décor.

416.

Check with the venue before planning your exit. A sparkler exit can be a dramatic way to end your wedding, but some venues won't allow anything that could pose a fire hazard. Check the rules before you light up. (And consider practicality. Even if your venue allows sparklers, is it the smartest thing to do in the middle of fire season in California?) Alternate exit ideas include glow wands, streamers, pennant flags, bubbles, eco-friendly confetti, and dried flowers.

417.

Use free printables for table décor. You don't need to spend money on table numbers or place settings for your wedding when there are tons of free printables online. Search for the item you're looking for, then browse designs and print them at home. (You can display printed table numbers in affordable frames for easy table décor.) And if you're not finding designs you love? Head to *Etsy* where you can buy professionally designed table numbers, seating charts, and other décor for around $5 to $10 each.

Easy DIY Favors Your Guests Will Actually Want

Forgoing favors is one of the easiest ways to trim your budget (your guests won't miss them), but if you like the idea of people taking home a parting gift (or if you're just looking for an excuse to craft), here are some easy DIY favors your guests will want to take home:

418. **A customized playlist.** You can easily share *Spotify* playlists using their built-in QR code maker. Download the code, then print one out for each guest. You can even get creative with designs and make it look like a mixtape.

419. **Anything edible.** Send your guests home with a late-night snack by packaging up doughnuts, chocolate-covered pretzels, cookies, caramel corn, or s'mores kits in to-go boxes.

420. **Homemade booze.** If you're a budding home brewer or have a killer limoncello recipe, bottle up your favorite alcohol in small containers and send one home with each guest.

421. **Oils, pickles, or salt.** If you and your partner are foodies, find an easy-to-replicate recipe for infused oils, seasoned salts, or pickled vegetables and package them up in mini glass containers.

422. **Jams or preserves.** If your family has a great recipe for preserved fruit, send guests home with a sample in the form of jam or jelly.

423. **Potted plants.** Potted greenery does double duty as both table décor and a take-home favor. Opt for mini versions of hardy plants like succulents that will survive the trip home.

424. Something local. If you're getting married in a location with distinct local flavors, give out a small sample to your guests as favors. Coffee beans, syrups, and honeys are ideal.

425. Soap. Mini custom soaps are equal parts practical and beautiful. If you're feeling especially crafty, you can make your own, or go the semi-DIY route with purchased soaps in DIY packaging.

426. Homemade hankies. Weddings are tearjerkers. Keep your guests prepared with customized handkerchiefs. Pass them out at the ceremony when they're needed most and your guests can keep them for the reception and beyond.

427. To-go boxes. If you have extra cake or sweets left over at the end of the party, you can turn dessert into a favor with clever to-go boxes. This is about as low-key as it gets.

428.

Get a display cake. Wedding cakes can get expensive (it takes a lot of work to pipe those decorations), but you can have all the beauty of an elaborate cake without the cost. If you're doing a traditional cake cutting, order a small display cake to cut and then supplement it with additional desserts for serving, like a sheet cake, cupcakes, cookies, or pie.

429.

Think beyond the cake. Don't like cake? Don't serve it! There are plenty of other dessert options that are just as appropriate. Wedding pie, macarons, cupcakes, or croquembouche can all make for lovely display options that are just as tasty as cake. You can also skip the sweets altogether and display a dessert alternative like a tower of cheese. (It's exactly what it sounds like. A stack of cheese wheels that looks like a wedding cake. You won't regret it.)

430.

Go for buttercream. Fondant makes for smooth, sculptural cakes, but it's more expensive to produce and takes more work to sculpt, so bakers usually charge an additional fee to work with it (sometimes $1 or more per slice). Opt for buttercream instead. Buttercream can still be smoothed out and decorated beautifully but it costs less (and people often prefer the taste anyway).

431.

Take your cake in the nude. Naked cakes are cakes with very little frosting around the outside (you've probably seen them all over *Pinterest*). Because they use less buttercream, they can be more affordable than other cakes, but there's another reason to consider an underdressed confection: They hold up better in heat. If it's going to be a scorcher on your wedding day, consider forgoing the elaborate frosting.

432.

Hack a grocery store cake. Many grocery store chains offer simple (and delicious) tiered wedding cakes at affordable prices. (You can also buy them à la carte and stack them yourself.) Just add fresh flowers and finish it off with a cool cake topper. You'll almost never know it wasn't a professionally crafted cake. Call your local grocery store (Costco is a good place to start) and see if they make wedding cakes in-house.

433.

Use toothpicks to keep flower stems out of your cake. Fresh flowers are an easy way to decorate your wedding cake, but you don't want to stick long stems into something your guests will be eating. (Even if it's an edible flower, it can negatively impact the flavor of your cake.) Instead, wrap your stems with floral tape or snap off the stems and stick toothpicks into the heads of the flowers, then proceed with decorating.

434.

Give your cake a little support. If you're stacking your own grocery store cakes or making a tiered cake from scratch, make sure your confection has enough internal support structures so it doesn't topple under its own weight. You can buy dowels from craft or home improvement stores or buy plastic cake supports online. (The plastic ones are easier to cut but might not be as strong.) As a general rule, the taller the cake, the more support you'll need.

435.

Serve up wedding cake in 1" slices. How many people your wedding cake will serve depends on how big you cut each slice. If you're working with a professional caterer, they should know how to serve cake to a crowd, but if you're serving your own slices, keep in mind that wedding cake servings are usually thinner than what you'd expect from something like birthday cake. Aim for a 1" width. If your guests are still hungry, they can always come back for seconds.

436.

Round down on cake servings. You don't need to have a slice of cake for every guest attending your wedding. Some people leave early; others will be too stuffed from dinner. Aim for about 15 percent fewer slices of cake than your total number of guests and you'll be in good shape. Just remember to factor in whether you'll be taking home some leftovers for yourselves.

437.

Decorate with greenery or herbs. Greenery can be a quick, easy, and affordable decorating tool. Buy bunches of herbs or filler greens and place small sprigs in your napkins or alongside your centerpieces. Organic décor is already a little rough around the edges, so if your tabletop ends up a little imperfect or uneven, it all contributes to the vibe.

438.

Give your guests something to do when they walk in. You don't need a professional guest wrangler at your wedding (adults should be able to entertain themselves during the quieter moments of the evening), but for those first few awkward moments upon arrival it's helpful to give people something to do to break the ice. This could include signing a guest book, enjoying passed hors d'oeuvres, taking advantage of a photo booth, or something as simple as finding their escort card and the accompanying table.

439.

Create luminaries from paper bags. DIY luminaries add affordable mood lighting to outdoor weddings. All you need is a white paper lunch bag, something to weigh it down (sand works well), and battery-operated candles. If you want a more decorative lighting element, you can also make DIY luminaries out of wax paper and pressed flowers, or water balloons dipped in melted wax. Use the search term "DIY luminaries" for inspiration and instructions.

440.

Use flameless candles in place of the real thing. Battery-operated candles can give your wedding ambiance even when your venue doesn't allow flames (and a pack of one hundred costs less than $25). When placed inside frosted glass, flickering tea lights can give the appearance of a real flame. Just double-check the battery life before you buy. You want to make sure your flameless candles last the duration of your reception.

441.

Add buffer time to your speeches. Instead of stacking toasts back-to-back, give your guests breathing room between speeches (you can spread them out between courses during dinner). That way your guests are just as interested in the third speech of the night as the first and they won't tune out during your BFF's tribute to you and your partner.

442.

Play tic-tac-toe with tape for floral arrangements. If you're making your own centerpieces, use this professional florist hack: Make a grid out of clear floral tape across the top of your vessel. The grid will help your flowers stay upright while you're arranging them and make it easy to remove and replace stems without disturbing the rest of the flowers around them. (You can get floral tape at most craft stores.) And don't worry if you can see a little bit of the tape on your vase. You can always cover that with greenery as you go.

443.

Use greenery to bolster your bouquet. Greenery is an affordable way to add volume to your flowers and is what makes those deconstructed, organic bouquets and arrangements look lush and expensive. If you're DIYing your own arrangements, start with the greenery first. It's easier to add in blooms after you've created a nest of greenery, and the foundation will help your flowers stay upright. FlowerMoxie.com has an easy tutorial on their *YouTube* channel that walks you through building an organic-looking bouquet starting with greenery.

444.

Paint the roses red. For a modern floral effect, paint the leaves of your greenery to match the color scheme of your bouquet. Design Master spray paint is safe to use on fresh and fake flowers and comes in a variety of bright, pastel, and metallic colors. Just make sure you hold the can far enough away from your flowers or greenery so it creates a fine mist and doesn't drip (15"–18" away ought to do it).

445.

Use bud vases to cover your table with flowers. Elaborate floral arrangements can be expensive. If you want flowers without the formality, place a single bloom and a bit of greenery inside a bud vase (you can find them for a dollar or two on party supply websites and at dollar stores), then stagger a few of those across your tables with some tea lights and you'll have plenty of ambiance to go around. Pro tip: If you vary the height of your flowers, it'll give your table more dimension.

446.

Don't discount the dollar store. The dollar store may evoke visions of kitschy plastic tchotchkes, but it's also an ideal place to source affordable DIY supplies like frames, candles, candle holders, ribbon, silk flowers, and vases. Hit up the online version at DollarTree.com to dig for stylish pieces you can buy in bulk.

447.

Go for faux in extreme heat. Heat and humidity are the enemies of wedding details. Heat can be particularly damaging to flowers and cakes, which tend to droop, sweat, and melt. If you know it's going to be really hot outside, opt for faux wherever you can. You can find multi-tiered faux cakes that look like the real thing on *Etsy* for as little as $30 to $50 and silk flowers at almost any craft store. You can even get professionally crafted silk floral arrangements from shops like SomethingBorrowedBlooms .com or TheFauxBouquets.com.

448.

Stay away from the fridge. If you're DIYing flowers, don't put them in the refrigerator. Commercial floral coolers are calibrated for flowers but the fridge you have in your home is more likely to damage blooms than keep them alive. Wholesale flowers ordered in bulk usually need a day or two to open up, and that's best done in a bucket of water in a cool, dry place. Read the fine print on floral care before you order any bulk supplies to make sure your flowers aren't especially sensitive to temperature or humidity (and consider opting for hardier flowers if they are).

449.

Take a picture of DIY décor. If you're having friends and family set up DIY décor, give them clear instructions for day-of assembly. Take an example photo of a finished product you've done yourself and include it with the materials needed for setup, so that your vision is clearly communicated and your helpers won't be left guessing on the day of (or worse, asking for logistical advice while you're busy getting dressed).

450.

Be cautious of paper and wind. If you're getting married outside, avoid delicate paper décor like trifold escort cards. If there's a gust of wind, your carefully placed details will go flying. Instead, use signage to tell your guests where to go and weigh down any essential paper goods (like programs) so they don't fly away.

451.

Have a load-in/load-out plan. All the details and décor you've planned for your wedding need a way to get into your venue and back out. If you haven't clearly identified who oversees that plan, it could well end up being you and your partner. (Hauling chairs is not a great way to end your wedding night.) Create a list of what items need to get transported to your venue (and by whom) and then who is responsible for getting them out (and how).

CHAPTER 6

Day-of Hacks

452.

Spend the night with your partner. Tradition says that couples should spend the night apart before the wedding (and if you want to, that's fine), but if you're going to be more anxious spending the night away from each other, do what's going to put you in the right emotional space to get married. There's also nothing that says you can't get ready together on the day of. Couples who do this often report feeling more relaxed leading up to the wedding itself.

453.

Print out a day-of checklist. In the hubbub of last-minute wedding prep, it's easy to forget basics that you might need on your wedding day, like your driver's license. Or deodorant. Make a day-of packing checklist a few days or even weeks before the wedding when you're in a clear headspace and tape it to your door or bathroom mirror the night before your wedding. Just remember to do a final inventory check before you leave the house!

454.

Pack an emergency kit. You never know when someone's shirt button is going to give out or if a bouquet ribbon will need last-minute reinforcing. Keep an emergency kit nearby throughout the day (ideally in someone's bag so you have supplies close by at all times). You can buy pre-assembled wedding emergency kits online, but the most important things to have handy include a mini sewing kit, safety pins, stain remover, ibuprofen or acetaminophen, fashion tape, a lint brush, breath mints, bobby pins, and hairspray (it fights static cling and flyaways).

455.

Know that something will go wrong. As with any complex event, the chances of something going wrong on your wedding day are high. This doesn't mean you need to prepare for disaster. Wedding day mishaps run the gamut from the wrong-colored napkins being delivered to no-show guests to inclement weather. While you can't predict and prevent the future, being emotionally prepared for snafus can make them easier to deal with on the day of.

456.

Travel with your outfits. If you're flying to your wedding location, don't mail your outfits to your destination. Instead, pack your outfits in your suitcases. You may have to compress them a bit to fit, but it's much easier to steam a wrinkled dress or suit than to find one that's gotten lost in the mail.

457.

Get grounded before the day starts. Weddings can be frenetic. There are a lot of people doing a lot of things at the same time. If you're normally introverted (and even if you're not), start your day with something that will ground you. Yoga. A long jog. A few laps around the pool. Whatever you normally do to feel present in your body and clear your mind. Even just a few minutes to meditate or journal can help start you off on the right foot.

458.

Don't forget a steamer. You don't want to be trying to iron out wrinkles on delicate fabrics like chiffon or silk in your hotel room while you're getting ready. A handheld steamer will set you back $30 to $40 and allow you to steam out wrinkles while clothes are on their hangers. (Just remember to check that the fabric won't be damaged by the moisture.) When the wedding is over, take the steamer home and it'll be a helpful tool in your closet.

459.

Keep snacks in the getting ready rooms. You'll probably get lots of advice about making sure to eat at the reception, but if there's going to be champagne flowing *before* the ceremony, keep plenty of filling snacks on hand so no one ends up tipsy before you even get to the venue. Include plenty of protein and lots of water to keep your energy up for the long day ahead.

460.

Wear your engagement ring on your right hand. You don't want to be fumbling around with your engagement ring while reciting your vows, so pop your engagement ring on your right hand at the beginning of the day. Your left hand will be kept clear for ceremonial ring exchanges and you won't be in danger of accidentally misplacing your engagement ring.

461.

Phone a friend. No one should be calling or texting you or your partner on the morning of the wedding (even well wishes can be overwhelming if you're not prepared to respond to a dozen texts), but well-meaning loved ones often forget this. Hand off your phone to your most trusted gatekeeper and let them handle any incoming texts or calls. You can also tape a note to the front of your getting ready door with alternate numbers to call if someone has an urgent last-minute need.

462.

Appoint an emotional bodyguard. Weddings don't always stop family drama, but that doesn't mean it should be yours to deal with on your wedding day. Ask one (or several) of your wedding party members or a trusted friend to serve as your emotional bodyguard and keep an eye out for any emerging issues. If they see trouble brewing, they can run interference before it ever gets back to you.

463.

Build bonus time into your schedule. A few people running ten minutes late or requesting changes to their hair and makeup can quickly turn into an hour-long delay. Build in extra time to your morning schedule to avoid being late or rushing. (At least an hour is a safe bet, particularly if you are getting hair and makeup done or have a large wedding party.) The worst-case scenario is you finish early, have extra time, and can chill with your loved ones without stressing.

464.

Use a crochet hook or bobby pin to fasten buttons. Those elaborate fabric buttons on the back of wedding dresses can take a while to close. Save your fingers some of the trouble and bring a bobby pin or crochet hook to the dressing room with you. Hook the curved end around the buttonhole loop and bring it over the button for a quicker and easier buttoning process. (Check out *YouTube* for video tutorials of how it's done.)

465.

Get your money's worth from your makeup. Do you normally struggle to choose cosmetic products? If you're hiring a professional hair or makeup artist, ask them to write down the name of every product and shade they used on you on your wedding day (and what skin care they would recommend for you too). You'll end up with an expertly tailored shopping list that you can take to the store.

466.

Ask someone to be your escape buddy. When checks have been cashed and flights have been booked, it's really hard to listen to the voice in your head telling you that you may not want to get married. But for some people, it happens! (Probably not you, but still.) Before the wedding, appoint a trusted confidante as your escape buddy. On the day of, their job is to double-check that you still want to do this thing. And if you don't? They'll have a taxi waiting in five minutes. Because it's always much better to cancel a wedding now than to get divorced later.

467.

Print or download tie tying instructions. There will inevitably be someone in your group who can't tie a tie (especially if your wedding party is donning bow ties), but in the event that *no one* remembers or can't agree on a preferred knot style, have instructions printed out or save an instructional video to your phone. (Don't rely on streaming. Rustic wedding venues have notoriously bad service.)

468.

Have a day-of lunch plan. You will need to eat on your wedding day, but that's an easy thing to forget when you're staring at a day-of schedule. Block out a forty-five-minute break for lunch and assign someone to be responsible for procuring the food. (Bonus: Being the lunch getter is one of those day-of tasks that can make an otherwise not included friend or family member feel like they have a special job.)

469.

Skip the limo. Renting a limo for your wedding serves two purposes: getting a large group of people from point A to point B and feeling fancy while doing it. If you only care about the former, skip the limo and arrange for alternate transportation. You can just as easily get to your venue in a handful of taxis or rideshares, saving hundreds of dollars in the process.

470.

Kick your wedding party out of the first look. First looks (when you stage a meeting with your partner before the wedding) are often intimate and emotional, but they are decidedly less so with ten of your closest friends around the corner heckling you and shouting "Aww!" Let your wedding party hang out in the hotel room or give them an alternate activity to do during the photo session to preserve the pre-wedding magic.

471.

Assign an official portrait wrangler. Wedding guests like to scatter after the ceremony, so getting them to show up for portraits can be like herding cats. Choose someone who *won't* be in any photos but recognizes your immediate family by face and name, then assign them to retrieve any VIPs needed for portraits.

Eleven Things Your Photographer Should Know on the Day Of

If you've chosen a photographer whose work you love, the best thing you can do on the day of is trust them to do their thing, but these eleven reminders will ensure they capture your day without a hitch:

472. **The dress code.** Let them know if there are any special circumstances that might impact their day-of uniform (challenging terrain, lots of walking, an extra formal affair) so they can plan.

473. **What you don't want.** Make sure your photographer knows if you'd prefer to get dressed without the paparazzi present or if there are sacred portions of your ceremony that should be left out of the coverage so they can put the camera down when needed.

474. **Your full timeline.** Your photographer should have all the details of your day ahead of time so they know where to be and when. They can also help optimize your schedule to make sure you have enough time for photos.

475. **Names for portraits.** If you put together a shot list, include five to ten of the most essential family portraits (such as your family all together, your partner's family all together, you and your partner with each set of parents), then include names so your photographer isn't shouting "Hey, green shirt! Can you move to the right?"

476. **Special guests.** If your uncle helped raise you, point him out to your photographer. Photographers don't always know who the non–wedding party VIPs are, and you don't want to end up with a bunch of photos of someone's plus-one.

477. **Family drama.** Is your cousin currently not speaking to the rest of the family? Is your parents' divorce still a sore wound? Your photographer can get creative with portrait order and help keep feuds to a minimum.

478. **Deceased loved ones.** Grief and weddings can be strange bedfellows. If you have a family member or special friend who has passed, help your photographer avoid any awkward situations or unintentional reminders by letting them know in advance.

479. **Out-of-order ceremony.** Most American weddings end with a kiss and a proclamation by the officiant, but sometimes (like in a traditional Catholic wedding) the order gets switched around. Let your photographer know if they should expect an important moment to show up early.

480. **Surprises.** If you're planning a flash mob, coordinating a sparkler exit, or otherwise going outside the box, let your photographer know when and where it's happening so they can be prepared with the right gear.

481. **Sentimental details.** Professional photographers usually do a good job of capturing the details you've put your time and energy into, but make sure to point out any family heirlooms or particularly important details so they can prioritize those first.

482. **If you're camera shy.** A good photographer will be a fly on the wall at your wedding, but tell them in advance if you're camera shy so they can work their magic as unobtrusively as possible.

483.

Maximize pre-ceremony portraits. Family portraits can eat up lots of precious cocktail hour time. If you plan on seeing your partner before the ceremony for a first-look photo, consider doing group portraits (like family and wedding party pictures) at the same time. There is more flexibility in the schedule pre-ceremony, plus you can get all the pesky formal pictures out of the way and enjoy more of your reception.

484.

Bring an invitation if you want it photographed. Wedding invitations are the one detail that don't usually make it to the event venue. If you spent a lot of time on yours or just want it documented in digital format, make sure to have one on hand the day of. Bring a copy to the getting ready room or, if you're afraid you'll forget, ask your photographer if you can mail it to them in advance.

485.

Ask for pictures you actually want. *Pinterest* shot lists are often filled with detail images, but staging photos means taking time away from photographing candids, so think about what's important to *you*. Do you care about a styled image of your wedding rings together? Your photographer might still capture it (there's a lot of downtime during the getting ready hours), but if it's not on your must-have list they're less likely to sacrifice quality candid moments for still life detail photos.

486.

Keep your photographer in the loop. Even if they have your timeline in hand, your photographer isn't going to be looking at their watch all night. Have someone give them a heads-up before anything important happens. Big dance? Important speech? Time to cut the cake? You'll want to make sure your photographer isn't in a different corner of the reception photographing something else and missing the action.

487.

Use your photographer's time wisely. If your photographer is covering a set number of hours during your wedding, maximize their reception coverage. Some of the best photos from weddings come from the last dance of the evening, so if your photographer can be there to capture it, all the better. Getting ready, on the other hand, is a lot of the same activity up until you get into your wedding outfit. You probably don't need three hours' worth of hair and makeup coverage.

488.

Consider which portraits you'll frame. Think about your walls after the wedding. Are you going to frame any photos of your family *without* your partner in them? Then consolidate your formal portraits to ones that include both you and your partner. Similarly, if you have a huge family, one large group photo may suffice over several small group photos. The more you consider which photos are likely to be framed in your home (or your parents' homes) after the wedding, the less likely you are to spend unnecessary time posing for pictures you don't need.

489.

Fake it 'til you make it in photos. Getting professional portraits taken can be awkward. If you feel uncomfortable, try faking it. Artificial laughter often turns into the real thing, and a good photographer will be able to capture the authentic moments. You can also try whispering silly things into your partner's ear. (Describing your favorite appetizer in a sultry whisper is a tried-and-true favorite.) When all else fails? Ignore your photographer altogether and focus on each other.

490.

Don't stuff your hands in your pockets. When getting formal portraits taken, take your hands out of your pockets. If you need to do something with your hands, put your fingers in your pockets with your thumbs draped over the side. It looks more natural and you can still see most of your hand.

491.

Let your photographer eat first. Once the ceremony is over, your photographer is going to be on their feet until the party ends. Give them an opportunity to rest while no one wants their photo taken: dinner. (No guest wants a mid-bite candid of themself.) If your photographer eats at the same time as your guests, they'll be able to get a full meal without needing to rush away to capture important toasts (or worse, accidentally missing them).

492.

Tell VIP guests to arrive twenty minutes early. If you want family members and friends in photos, tell them to arrive fifteen to twenty minutes before you actually need them. That way, if everyone shows up on time, you're twenty minutes ahead of schedule. In the more likely event that someone runs late, your day-of timeline won't get thrown out of whack.

493.

Help your guests find their way. If your wedding is in a complicated location (or if there are multiple weddings in the same place that
day), set up signage to direct your guests to the appropriate areas. Have
more complicated logistics, like an island wedding that requires a ferry?
Appoint helpers to direct traffic or pass out tickets so no one gets lost.

494.

You don't need a welcome sign. Unless you want a welcome sign in
your home after the wedding, you can skip this piece of décor. Walking
into your reception will be all the welcome your guests need and it'll be
one less thing to sort out once the wedding is over.

495.

Start the ceremony late. It's all but guaranteed there will be at least one latecomer to your ceremony (whether because of traffic, getting lost, or miscalculating travel time). Plan on starting your ceremony ten to fifteen minutes late to account for stragglers. If it's built into the plan from day one, you won't be as anxious when you're staring out at a sea of guests waiting for things to start. (Just don't tell your guests you plan on starting late!)

496.

Invite your community into your ceremony. If you can get your guests emotionally invested in your ceremony, they'll ride that emotional high well into the reception (leading to a pretty great party). Invite your guests into the ritual by including them in something interactive like a ring warming (where every guest handles your rings before you put them on) or a group statement supporting your commitment to each other.

497.

Rent sound equipment for the ceremony. Even with the best acoustics, your venue might not enable your guests in the back to hear your ceremony clearly (which really takes the zing out of things). If your ceremony venue doesn't have built-in sound equipment, consider renting. You can get a simple audio setup from your local event rental company starting at around $100 to $150 (suitable for up to one hundred guests). Rentals usually include speakers and microphones, with upgrades for wireless or wearable mics. Just remember to ask if a mic stand is included so you can put the mic down when you're not using it.

498.

Speak and walk slowly at the ceremony. If you're a fast walker or talker, slow it down for the ceremony (especially if nerves are likely to make you speed up). Aim for a pace that's about three-quarters your normal speed. The best way to figure out the ideal timing of your ceremony is to have a rehearsal before the wedding. There you can correct a speedy walk or hard-to-understand vows.

499.

Tape your vows into a favorite book. A folded piece of paper or note card doesn't really scream "formal event," but that's what most people end up with when reading their vows. It's certainly not the end of the world, but if you don't have yours memorized and you want something that looks nice in photos, tape or paste your vows into a pretty notebook, journal, or a piece of meaningful literature.

500.

Record your vows. You don't need a professional videographer to immortalize your vows. Set up a phone or DSLR camera with video capabilities on a tripod and instruct someone to hit record at the beginning of your ceremony. It might not be a professional-quality recording, but in five or ten years when you want to wax nostalgic you probably won't care.

501.

Keep your guests cool and hydrated. Outdoor summer ceremonies can become dangerous if it gets too hot. (Guests don't always remember to hydrate while getting ready, and the earlier arrivals can be waiting around for an hour in the sun.) To avoid dehydration, consider offering water as your guests arrive. It doesn't have to be pretty or fancy; this one's all about function. You can also provide programs that double as paper fans to help people stay cool during the festivities.

502.

Hold your bouquet with your wrists at your hips. Holding a bouquet never feels natural. To avoid holding it too high or too low, place your wrists at your hips then tilt the bouquet slightly outward. This keeps your arrangement in a neutral position that won't block your outfit while also showcasing the flowers that make up the body of the bouquet.

503.

Hold your kiss for a few seconds. If an iconic first kiss photo is an important part of your must-have photo list, don't peck your partner and then pull away quickly during the ceremony. (Cameras don't always work that fast!) Make sure to linger for a few seconds to give your photographer ample time to capture the romance.

Ten Wedding Planner Hacks You Want for the Day Of

There are some things you learn only when you've been behind the scenes at a ton of weddings. These are the things professional wedding planners wish you knew before saying "I do."

504. Pack a white paint marker. Stain removers or bleach might remove stains from white fabric, but they also leave large wet marks. In a pinch, use a white paint pen (found at craft stores) to cover any stains.

505. Use tape in lieu of a bra. Most wedding dresses have built-in support structures, but if you need a little more life or coverage in a low-back or plunging gown, body tape, boob tape, or nude gaffer tape will do the job. Stick a roll in your to-go bag just in case.

506. Bring a backup outfit. Wine happens. If you end up with a stain on your shirt or dress (or are uncomfortable in a big ball gown toward the end of the night), keep a change of clothes nearby. And don't forget a spare pair of socks!

507. Don't leave without paying your vendors. At the beginning of the day, hand your final checks and tips to a trusted friend to ensure that payments get delivered before the night is over (and that you're not making a return trip to the venue to do it at 11 p.m.).

508. Remember your meds. Life happens, even at weddings. When packing for your wedding night, be sure to include your medications, and keep any emergency supplies close by at the reception (like your EpiPen).

509. **Seal and send your marriage certificate.** If you sign your wedding certificate on your wedding day, have an envelope ready (with postage), then slip it into the nearest mailbox on your way out the door. You don't want to end your wedding without the legal paperwork.

510. **Call ahead for late hotel check-in.** If you're going to be arriving at a hotel after your wedding, make sure they accept late check-ins when you book your room and call ahead on the morning of to remind them you'll be arriving late. The last thing you want is to end up stranded at the reception desk at midnight.

511. **Remove hair ties.** If you don't want hair ties showing up in all your wedding photos, do a wrist check before leaving for the ceremony, and make sure your wedding party removes theirs.

512. **Test your guest book pen.** If you're having a guest book that involves guest signatures, test your pen ahead of time to make sure it doesn't smudge. An ultra-fine Sharpie should do the trick.

513. **Have someone pack you a to-go box.** It's hard to get in a full meal at your wedding. Have someone prepare a to-go box of your wedding food so you can snack on it later from the comfort of your bed.

514.

Ask your guests to put away their phones. Thanks to overzealous guests who think they're Ansel Adams with an iPhone, unplugged (aka, phone-free) ceremonies are becoming more standard. If you're worried about shutter-happy guests, have your officiant make an announcement at the beginning of your ceremony that you want your guests to be able to experience the ceremony with as much presence as possible so you've hired a professional wedding photographer to capture every moment, and that you kindly request they put their cell phones away. This usually does the trick.

515.

Have a backup plan for children in the ceremony. If you're involving a child in your ceremony and that child is under the age of six, have a backup plan in case the pressure of the job gets to be too much. The backup plan can be a parent escort or simply speeding up the ceremony to skip over their part.

516.

Use a wagon to escort very small children. Have older children pull smaller ones down the aisle in a small wagon. It gives older kids a place to focus their efforts while taking the pressure off toddlers who might not be ready to walk down an aisle unassisted. (Plus, it makes for a cute photo op.) Just be sure the smaller participants are old enough to sit up confidently and won't topple over (or you could decorate a wagon that's outfitted with baby seats in it).

517.

Get a babysitter. If you're inviting a lot of kids to the wedding (particularly if they're traveling from out of town), consider hiring an onsite caretaker who can watch the little ones after dinner, that way the parents can stay for the whole event without having to cut out early for bedtime. Just make sure you communicate this plan early and understand if people decline. Some parents will jump at the opportunity for a free night out while others may want to keep their kids close by regardless.

518.

Confetti makes everything better. You don't need a ton of décor or fancy details to make important moments pop on camera. Just add confetti! A little confetti during your first kiss, recessional, on the steps of your venue after the ceremony, or anywhere else that you'll be celebrating will add instant party energy to your photos. (Plus, it gets your guests in on the action.) Just remember to check if your venue allows confetti, and make sure you have a cleanup plan.

519.

Opt for eco-friendly confetti outdoors. If you want to use confetti outside, avoid littering and use an alternative instead, like dried herbs or flowers. If you want the look of more traditional party confetti, TheConfettiBar.com has colorful, biodegradable confetti that you can purchase by the bag or in bulk. You can even customize it with your preferred color scheme.

520.

Take fifteen minutes for yourself (and your partner). It's easy for your wedding day to fly by, but you didn't spend a year planning just to skip to the end of the party! Grab your partner and take fifteen minutes to be alone after your ceremony and soak in the joy of the commitment the two of you just made. It will give you a chance to re-energize and center yourselves before going back to enjoy the rest of the celebration.

521.

Don't sneak into your reception. If being the center of attention overwhelms you, you might be tempted to sneak into your reception instead of being announced. But, without the formality of an announcement, you're actually more likely to be swarmed by guests the second you walk through the door. If you want some space, have someone announce your entrance (typically your DJ if you have one) and then head right to your sweetheart or head table to have a seat.

522.

Provide baskets of essentials. The bathroom basket is a familiar staple at weddings (usually containing feminine hygiene products, floss or toothpicks, bobby pins, a small hairspray bottle, and anything else that might come in handy during a dance party), but if you're getting married outdoors or in the summertime, seasonal essentials can protect your guests against the unexpected. (Most of your guests won't remember to pack sunscreen or bug spray with their cocktail attire.)

523.

Remember to eat something. Receptions can go by very quickly. Between portraits, toasts, and dancing, it's surprisingly easy to forget to feed yourself (especially if you're making the rounds during dinnertime when everyone is seated). Designate someone (a friend, your coordinator, a member of your wedding party) to make a plate of food for you and your partner so you don't forget to eat. Even better: Take that plate of food and sneak away for a quick break to relax and hang out with your partner before going back to partying.

524.

Use wine wipes to avoid mouth stains. You will never be photographed more than you will on your wedding day. If you're worried about wine stains around your mouth or on your teeth and then having those stains show up in photos, purchase a set of wine wipes. The specially formulated wipes can be rubbed along your mouth and teeth without leaving any residual flavor (so you can keep on sippin'). Stash a packet in your purse or pocket.

525.

Keep toasts to three minutes (or less). When given free rein, people's understanding of what constitutes a toast can run the gamut. Suggest speakers keep it under three minutes (which is about the length of most guests' attention spans), and while you don't want to dictate too much of what your loved ones put in their speeches, this is a good time to remind them that a wedding is not the right place to test out their budding stand-up skills. Keep it short, sweet, and thoughtful.

526.

Don't put your gift table out front. If you've got a gift table with a card box, keep it away from the entrance of your party. It's not often that wedding crashers will nab your gifts, but it makes it much easier for someone to get away with your cash if the card box is close to the door.

527.

Remember to tip your vendors. Some of your vendors (catering, for example) may include a built-in service charge with their base fee, but if you want to tip above and beyond, here's a helpful hint: Tipping is considered standard for all service professionals who don't own the business they work for (drivers, setup crew, photographers or coordinators who are part of a larger studio, and catering staff if it's not already included in the bill). Hair and makeup should also be tipped. Most other cases are considered optional.

528.

Review if you can't tip. If you want to show your vendors love beyond a tip, a heartfelt gift or card can go a long way (*if* you have a personal relationship with the vendor; your driver probably just wants cash), but one of the best ways you can support wedding professionals is to leave a positive review of their business on sites like WeddingWire.com, TheKnot .com, *Yelp*, or *Google*. Or refer new business to them by word of mouth. Future clients are worth much more than a $50 bill.

529.

Ask your caterer if you can donate unused food. Professional caterers are pretty good at estimating how much food your guests will need, but you'll probably still end up with some leftovers. After packing a to-go box for yourself, ask your venue if they can pack up your leftovers to pass out to any homeless residents in the area. (If you have a professional wedding coordinator, this might be something you can work out with them in advance as you will probably be spending your post-wedding hours…asleep.) This prevents the food from going to waste while offering a high-quality hot meal to those in need.

530.

Let your guests take the décor. If you are planning on discarding your décor after the wedding (especially fresh flowers), alleviate the task by letting your guests take it home. Your centerpieces can have a second life adorning your great aunt's coffee table while serving as a happy reminder of your joyful wedding, and it's one less thing for your haul-out crew to contend with.

531.

Don't toss your décor. If you're incorporating something meaningful into your wedding, consider how you might be able to bring it home after the fact. For example, if you're smashing a glass as part of a Jewish wedding, can you repurpose the shards to create a mezuzah for your home? Or if you're jumping the broom, can you find space in your home for that broom as décor? When the wedding is over, it's nice to have a reminder of the day that also serves a practical purpose in your everyday lives.

532.

Throw the bouquet up and out. If you opt to throw a bouquet, try to throw it up and away from your body. If you throw it straight up into the air, it's going to land a few feet away from you and your guests will need to make a run for it, so give that bouquet a nice arc and a lot of muscle. Another way to make the bouquet toss more fun? Instead of singling out unmarried folks, make it an inclusive event for anyone who wants to join in.

533.

Pass around a Polaroid. Instead of a photo booth, pick up a Polaroid or Fujifilm Instax camera and a bunch of instant film packs. Leave the camera and film near your guest book or pass the Polaroid around to your guests and encourage everyone to take candids throughout the evening. Guests can keep a favorite photo for themselves as a favor and tape one into your guest book as a fun addition to their signature.

534.

Assign someone to return rentals. If you've rented anything à la carte that needs to be returned in person after the wedding (such as sound equipment), ask a close friend or relative if they can own the task of bringing it back. After the joy and exhaustion of your wedding day, you won't want to be hauling equipment back to the rental store (or getting so carried away in the post-wedding glow that you forget).

535.

Pace yourselves. The combination of a fast-moving event with lots of activity and free-flowing booze means it's very easy to get drunk at your wedding without even realizing it's happening, so mind your tolerance and pace yourself throughout the evening. Follow each drink with a glass of water and keep snacks handy so you're not in bed before the party's over. (It happens more often than you think.)

536.

Bring a clear umbrella. If the forecast calls for rain, pack a clear umbrella in your emergency kit. Clear umbrellas make it easier to see your face in photos without the shadow a darker umbrella might cast. You can find clear bubble umbrellas for around $15 at stores like Target and Walmart, or buy them in bulk online if you want your entire wedding party covered.

537.

Take a two-day mini-moon to rest. You need a break after your wedding to process the emotional high of the event (and to recuperate from all the work that went into it). If you're planning a delayed honeymoon, it can be tempting to head right back to work to maximize future paid time off, but wedding burnout makes for a grumpy employee. Even if you can't take a formal honeymoon right after the wedding, take a day or two off just to relax. Go to the next town over, check into a hotel, and don't move for forty-eight hours. It's almost as good as the beach.

538.

Resell your décor to recoup costs. There's no guarantee you'll be able to offload your wedding décor once the fun is over (always have a backup plan), but that doesn't mean you can't try! Use the ONBB app or sites like Tradesy.com. You can also try *Facebook Marketplace*, *Craigslist*, or *The Knot*'s classified pages to find local buyers for your wedding goods. However, your best bet is to find someone in your network who's getting married after you and ask if they'd like to purchase your décor.

539.

Don't feel bad if you don't consummate the marriage. There's a lot of pressure to have sex on your wedding night, but at the end of a fourteen-hour day (give or take), you're going to be really tired. If you do manage to get down to business after all that? Great! If not? It doesn't mean anything about your relationship (other than you probably had a really fun and exhausting party).

540.

Tell everyone you're newlyweds. When you check into your hotel room or if you grab a bite to eat the day after your wedding, let people know you're newlyweds. Most folks are glad to celebrate a recently married couple, and you may find yourself on the receiving end of a few free perks. Hello, celebratory bottle of champagne!